The Saga of the Paddy's Run

Thomas Jefferson, President of the United States of America,

TO ALL TO WHOM THESE PRESENTS SHALL COME, GREETING:

Know Ye, That Edward Bell, of Hamilton county, Ohio, having deposited in the Treasury a certificate of the Register of the Land-office at Cincinnati, whereby it appears that _____ full payment [?] for the West half of Lot or Section number Twenty-three of Township number Three _____ of Range number two of [?] _____ of the Lands directed to be sold at Cincinnati _____, "An act providing for the sale of the Lands of the United States in the Territory northwest of the Ohio, and above the mouth of Kentucky river," and of the acts amendatory of the same, **There is granted**, by the United States, unto the said Edward Bell _____, the ex section _____ of land above described: **To have and to hold** the said half _____ _____ of land, with the appurtenances, unto the said Edward Bell h[is] _____ heirs and assigns forever.

In testimony whereof, I have caused these Letters to be made **Patent**, and the Seal of the United States to be hereunto affixed.

Given under my Hand at the City of Washington, the ____ day of ____ in the year of our Lord one thousand eight hundred and ____ and of the Independence of the United States of America, the ____.

BY THE PRESIDENT,

Th: Jefferson

James Madison
Secretary of State.

Deed for the first land sold in the present Morgan Township, Butler County, to the first settler of the first Welsh settlement in Ohio. Signed by Thomas Jefferson April 5, 1806.

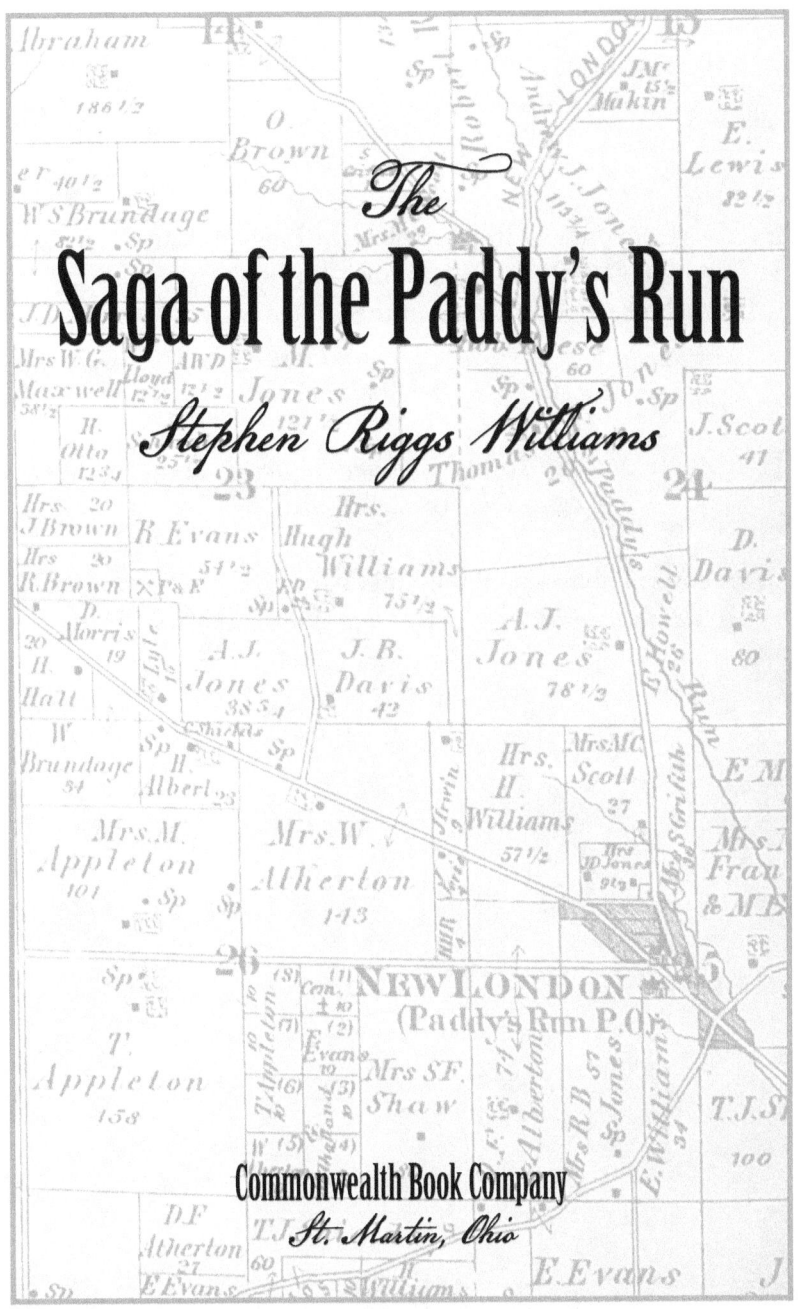

Saga of the Paddy's Run
Stephen Riggs Williams

Commonwealth Book Company
St. Martin, Ohio

Copyright © 1945 by Stephen Riggs Williams.
Copyright © 2020 by Commonwealth Book Company, Inc.
All rights reserved. Printed in the United States of America.

ISBN: 978-1-948986-22-9

Front cover: Morgan Township, *Combination Atlas Map of Butler County Ohio* (Philadelphia, 1875).

Back cover: Public school building, New London, *Combination Atlas Map of Butler County Ohio* (Philadelphia, 1875).

*To Abner and
Martha Ann Vaughan
Francis (my uncle and aunt)
who took me into their family
when my parents returned to
their mission work in China*

PREFACE

The Paddy's Run history, planned by my uncle, Roger Williams, Miami 1872, but never completed as he died in 1873, was prefaced as follows:

"The publication of this work calls for no apology from its author. He has long since deplored the fact that no records of the early settlement and subsequent growth of Paddy's Run have been preserved; and, fearing lest the barest outlines even of its early history may pass into oblivion unless the present opportunity be improved while there are still a few pioneers among us, he has undertaken the publication of this work, trusting that it may be favorably received by its readers, and only regretting that the task of compilation has not been performed by abler hands."

This seventy-three year old preface seems still appropriate in 1945. All the pioneers and all of their children are gone. Mr. Chidlaw's historical address of July 30, 1876, based to a great extent on the manuscript left by Roger Williams, is included as an appendix to the present volume, which is an endeavor to present to date the results of the lives of these earnest settlers in a small frontier community, by a history of their descendants, now, one hundred and fifty years later, scattered over the United States, upholding the principles taught by the fathers in this early training school for citizenship.

As may be seen by the list of collaborators, this history is almost a community affair, and I wish to thank all who have helped in so many ways.

I wish, also, to thank the President and Secretary of Miami University for the assignment of a sum of money, given by Dr. Albert Shaw in 1929 toward the history of the influence of some local settlement in the Miami Valley on the development of our country, to this study of the first Welsh settlement in Ohio.

Stephen R. Williams

TABLE OF CONTENTS

CHAPTER		PAGE
I.	The Saga of the Paddy's Run (Ohio Journal of Science, Vol. 41, No. 4)	15
II.	Early Days:	
	The Wild Animals	31
	Contacts with the Indians	33
III.	Implements, House and Farm:	
	Soap Day	38
	The Blacksmith Shop	39
IV.	1818 Immigrants and Morgan Gwilym's Letter to Wales	41
V.	The 1828 Squirrel Hunt, *by Flora Shields*	45
VI.	The Migration to Gomer, 1833	49
VII.	Earthquakes and Meteorites:	
	The 1811-12 Earthquakes	51
	The 1833 Meteorites, *by Murat Halstead and John Vaughan, Jr.*	51
VIII.	The Asiatic Cholera, 1834	54
IX.	Early Cabinet Makers	63
X.	The Roads, the Pike and the Bus	71
XI.	The Militia:	
	The War of 1812 (also see Appendix III)	77
	The Mexican War	78
	The Civil War (also see Appendix III)	78
	Soldiers of World War I (see Appendix I)	166
	Soldiers of World War II (see Appendix I)	166
XII.	Names of the Paddy's Run Postoffice	83
XIII.	Sons and Daughters of the Community	89
XIV.	Special Biographies	105

CHAPTER		PAGE
XV.	The Old Graveyard and the Churches:	
	The Old Graveyard, by S. R. Williams and Annie F. Crafts	113
	The Community House, by Edith Morris	117
	The Catholic Church, by Thomas Scheel	119
	The United Brethren Church, by Edna Walther and Ruth W. Wilson	119
	The Congregational Church from 1856, by Clara Francis	120
XVI.	The Schoolhouses of Paddy's Run	127
XVII.	The Libraries of Paddy's Run, by Martha Francis and S. R. Williams	131
XVIII.	Houses:	
	The John Vaughan House	139
	The James Shields House, by Clara Francis	141
	The Halstead Houses, by Alice Scott Robinson	144
	The Hewn Loghouse of the Thomas Select School, by Mr. and Mrs. Paul Robinson	146
	The John Evans House, by Lela Evans Walther	150
	The Birthplace of Albert Shaw	153
	The Dan Wilkins House, by Clara Wilkins Irwin	154
	The (Butterfield) Morris House, by Edith Morris	157
	The Abner Francis House	160
	Appendix I. Lists of Soldiers in World Wars 1, 2	166
	Appendix II. Articles of Faith. Constitution and History of the Congregational Church of the Whitewater, by the Rev. B. W. Chidlaw, 1840	167
	Appendix III. Historical Sketch of Paddy's Run, by the Rev. B. W. Chidlaw, July 30, 1876	172
	Bibliography	192
	Index	193

LIST OF COLLABORATORS

The Francis Family
Miss Edith and Mr. Crawford Morris
Mr. and Mrs. Henry H. Robinson
Mr. and Mrs. Henry Halstead Robinson
Mr. Clarence Jones
Dr. Albert Shaw
Mr. Thomas J. J. Scheel
Mr. and Mrs. Roger Evans
Mr. and Mrs. Raymond Irwin
Mr. and Mrs. Paul Robinson
Miss Edna Walther and Mrs. Ruth W. Wilson
Mrs. Fred Walther
Mrs. Margaret Jones Spicer, Wilmington, Delaware
Miss Anne Peate, Gomer, Ohio
Mrs. Martha Adams, Greensburg, Indiana
Mrs. Bernice M. Woodhams, Kalamazoo, Michigan
Mr. Ray Evans, Lima, Ohio
Mrs. Robert Mann, Oxford Ohio

CHAPTER I

THE SAGA OF THE PADDY'S RUN

Presidential address by Stephen Riggs Williams given at the fifty-first annual meeting of the Ohio Academy of Science. Reprinted from the Ohio Journal of Science, Vol. XLI, No. 4, July, 1941.

THINKING over the varied interests of our Academy audience, and the infinitesimal area in the field of zoology in which I might claim original knowledge, it seemed evident that were I to speak along that line tonight it would bore even the other zoologists.

There is, however, a matter of history which should interest you all as members of the Commonwealth of Ohio, which I have had especial opportunities to study from original sources. They say every man who is born has one speech in his make-up and I hope for your sakes that this is mine.

You realize that we all have a good knowledge of the things of the present, and a fraction of what went on forty years ago which our parents knew. By the time we get to our grandparents, our fraction of their unwritten knowledge is a small one, and when it comes to great-grandparents, unless it has been written down where it may be read, one is exceptional if he knows the names of those eight persons, and can make a fifty per cent grade in answering the questions as to where they were born or married, or of what they died.

The modifications which produced the stage on which this history of the Paddy's Run Valley was enacted have been taken from the "Bulletin on the Geology of Cincinnati" by Professor N. M. Fenneman.

THE PADDY'S RUN VALLEY

Preparation of the valley for the first settlers dates back to the time of the receding Wisconsin glaciation, perhaps 20,000 years ago. In the interglacial period between the Illinoian and Wisconsin ice sheets the Whitewater River, now a tributary to the Miami, emptied into the ancestral Ohio near the city of Harrison in Hamilton County. The old Ohio made an enormous north bend in the present city of Cincinnati, flowing northward through the present Mill Creek Valley to Symmes Corner in Butler County, where the larger Miami entered it and the combined rivers bore off southwest toward New Haven and Harrison and beyond.

As the Wisconsin ice spread over the northwest two-thirds of Ohio, the water melting from it formed a succession of long pools marking the bed of the present Ohio River. The lower end of one of these pools was at Anderson's Ferry just west of Cincinnati. Following the course of two small streams, one flowing eastward toward Cincinnati and the other on the opposite side of the divide flowing toward the ancestral river south of Harrison, the accumulation of water cut through the hills and thereby eliminated the enormous Mill Creek-Symmes Corner-Harrison northward bend, giving us the present course of the Ohio River from Cincinnati to Lawrenceburg.

As the ice mass withdrew very slowly over the Symmes Corner-Harrison section of the ancestral river, by utilizing the valleys of certain small streams to the east and south of the ice front, the flood water cut a path from below Venice, by New Baltimore and Miamitown to the region of Cleves. This has been used by the Great Miami, whose waters follow first the old valley from Symmes Corner, then this narrower new valley to Cleves, and then are joined by the Whitewater from the north to reach the straightened Ohio below Elizabethtown.

This same lingering of the ice mass caused the stream now known as the Dry Fork of the Whitewater, which had entered the ancestral Ohio independently at Fernald, to skirt the ice and cut southward through a ridge, thereby reaching the Ohio bed much farther west and now emptying into the Whitewater River below Harrison. This new lower end of this stream runs over the thick deposit of gravel in the ancestral valley and as a consequence, except at flood times, the visible water is so much reduced that the early settlers called it the Dry Fork (of the Whitewater). The narrow, deep, steep incline of the cut through the ridge just mentioned was well adapted for an inexpensive mill dam and a short mill race, and here the first grist mill for the earliest settlers was located. The unused lower part of the old Dry Fork, together with the shorter branches from the east and north now forms a smaller separate stream entering the Miami below Fernald near where the newer narrow post-glacial part of the Miami Valley begins. This is the Paddy's Run.

I cannot do better than to quote from Murat Halstead's picture of the Paddy's Run valley:

"The bosom of the valley was laced with a thread of silver; a stream—the home of sunfish—murmured and sparkled under lofty sycamores, statuesque, their arms white as marble, and lowly willows that drooped along the shining water like slender rods of gold.... The springs at the foot of the hills could be traced like veins in a leaf as little brooks to the larger stream in the center, that brightening with their increase, babbled over the polished gravel and glistening sand southward to the Great Miami and the greater and splendid Ohio."

No one knows whether the luckless Irishman—possibly one of Wayne's scouts—whose name the valley bears, actually was drowned or merely engulfed in the semi-liquid mud as he crossed the run following the west bank of the Miami north toward Hamilton. But the stream was named in his honor and later the postoffice of the same name in the village farther upstream was so distinctive that letters from Wales addressed to Paddy's Run, America, arrived safely.

THE INDIANS

In traditional times no Miami Indians lived the year round in this valley. They knew Kentucky as the Dark and Bloody Ground, and planned to spend their winters at least two days march north of the Ohio so as to avoid surprise attacks.

The narrow beaten paths through the woods along the tops of the hills possibly date back to the post-glacial mammoths and mastodons whose bones two centuries ago gave the name to Big Bone Lick on the Kentucky side of the river below Lawrenceburg. These paths were certainly used by the buffalo (bison) as they made their way from one prairie opening or windfall to another. The explanation for the single file habitual to Indian war parties is that they followed these paths on their march.

Old Chief Kiatta and his daughter, Okeana, left their names—the one for a small tributary of Dry Fork, Kiatta Creek, and the other for the present village of Okeana in the center of Morgan Township, both near their summer residence on Camp Run.

Indians were not uncommon sights to the white settlers until after the wholesale deportations beyond the Mississippi in the 1820's. Many of you have driven through Miami, Oklahoma, a name which is a monument to the forced migration of one particular tribe.

The Welsh Immigration

A majority of the early white settlers in the Paddy's Run valley were Welsh. In 1795 a party of emigrants started from Llanbrynmair, Montgomeryshire, North Wales. Among them were George Roberts and wife, David and Mary Francis, the Rev. Rees Lloyd, wife, and children, and two young unmarried men, Edward Bebb and Ezekiel Hughes. They had planned to be transferred by sail boat from the nearest point on Cardigan Bay to Bristol and there embark on the ship Maria for Philadelphia. For fear of the press-gang it was decided that the women only should sail with the luggage while the men, for safety's sake to avoid impressment as sailors, would walk the fifty or sixty miles to Bristol. Something delayed the expected freight boat a number of days. The alarmed women walked twenty miles toward Bristol and met the men coming back to find out what was the matter. The boat with the baggage must have come along and picked up the whole party because they reached the Maria at the last moment, after they had been given up and the ship was about to start without them.

Landing at Philadelphia, the party scattered. George Roberts and Rees Lloyd and their families settled at Ebensburg, Cambria County, near the center of Pennsylvania; the Francises stopped near Philadelphia; while Bebb and Hughes, having no families, continued westward to Cincinnati, arriving in 1796.

The Symmes Purchase land had been picked over and the land west of the Great Miami, not yet surveyed, was not on the market. There was nothing to do but wait. Ezekiel Hughes bought 100 acres in Section 34 on Blue Rock Creek in Colerain Township, which, though in the Symmes Purchase, was so rough and broken as not to be in demand. Others of the Welsh families stopped in Blue Rock later for the same reason, and the first white child born in Colerain Township was to one of these families.

When the surveyed lands were available in 1801, Bebb bought half a section on the Dry Fork of the Whitewater in Butler County, while Ezekiel Hughes, being more of a plutocrat, bought two sections further south in Hamilton County. Since neither of these men was married, they started, as soon as the farms were arranged for, on the long journey back to Wales for helpmeets.

Hughes, back home in Wales, married a Margaret Bebb, who may have been a sister of his friend Edward Bebb. To tell the Bebb story I shall have to leave Bebb and Hughes trudging along the roads eastward, and start back in Wales myself.

No letter, as far as we know, had come back from America during the years from 1795 to 1801 while the immigrants were waiting for their land, and it may have been thought that the young fellows were dead. As a result Margaret Roberts, sister of George Roberts of the 1795 party, who had known Edward Bebb when they were children, had been urged by her family into marrying a Rev. Mr. Owens. Her older sister, Grace, her husband and two children were planning to emigrate to America, and the Rev. Mr. Owens and his bride decided to accompany them. They started in 1801; the passage was long and tempestuous. Both husbands and Grace's two children died, reportedly from bad water, and were buried at sea. Another version of the story is that the captain and mate of the vessel, taking note of the two beautiful young women, took pains to poison the water for the unwanted relatives. At any rate, the two widowed sisters are said to have left the ship secretly at the Philadelphia dock by sliding down a rope at the bow while the officers were superintending the regular debarkation. They made their way to their brother, George Roberts at Ebensburg, sending a messenger back to the ship to claim their abandoned belongings.

Believe it or not, two days after Margaret Roberts Owens reached Ebensburg, her childhood acquaintance, Edward Bebb, walked in from his farm on Dry Fork. It did not take him long to decide not to go any farther toward Wales. He and Mrs. Owens were married February 2, 1802, probably walked to Pittsburgh, certainly floated from there to Cincinnati on a flatboat or broad-horn and reached the Dry Fork in time for Edward to do some spring planting. (The two-story log house in which the Bebbs set up housekeeping is still in use.) On December 8, 1802, William Bebb, one of the subjects of this paper, was born.

Forming the Community

For more than twenty years a stream of Welsh came to the Paddy's Run, and from it as the country opened, other Welsh settlements were made, notably in the regions of the headwaters of the Miami, Maumee, and Wabash from which the Indians had been sent west.

With neighbors helping, a comfortable log cabin could be built in two days and the amount of food obtainable was limited only by the rate of clearing the land.

Others appreciated the fertile soil of the Paddy's Run valley besides the numerous Welsh whom I have not attempted to name. Appleton, Blackburn, Carmack, Drybread, Halstead, Harding, Howard, Milholland, Parkinson, Phillis, and Shaw are names of families from the older states who settled in and about the valley.

James Shields, Glasgow University graduate, was for many years the representative for Butler County in Columbus, and at least once was the district Representative in the capital at Washington.

Church

After the settling, the first endeavor as a community was to start a church society. This was in 1803, the year Ohio became a state. The incoming Welsh were usually non-conformists or dissenters from the English Established Church. Those from the eastern states probably represented many different forms of worship. The story goes that the committee of five who drafted a church constitution were of five different church persuasions and that they chose the Congregational type because it was self-governing and because it was a church not represented by any committeeman.

Services were held at the cabins of different members, in a private school house, in a wagon-maker's shop, and in favorable seasons in a grove of sugar maples. By 1825 a brick meeting house, now the community house, was erected in this grove.

School

The first school was established in 1807, long before Ohio's public schools began to operate. The teacher boarded around in the homes from which the children came, and received in addition an honorarium of $0.75 per week.

In 1809 a subscription school charging $1.50 per child for a term of three months was started. Students learned reading, writing, and arithmetic, graduating at the Rule of Three.

In 1819 David Lloyd, a graduate of the University of Pennsylvania, introduced grammar and geography, and separated his students into groups or classes. A letter from William Bebb to his sister, Mrs. Vaughan, speaks of the high quality of Lloyd's teaching. He must have had a screw loose somewhere, however, as he is said to have spent most of his life trying to devise a perpetual motion machine.

In 1821 the Rev. Thomas Thomas established a high school and boarding school in which he taught to advanced pupils grammar, geography, arithmetic, algebra and geometry.

Library

In 1821 a bill was passed in the Ohio Legislature incorporating the Union Library Association of Morgan and Crosby Townships. Sixty-five shares costing $3.00 each were sold. The books were kept at a grist mill at the Dry Fork Cut previously mentioned because every family had to bring wheat and corn there to be ground.

When the turnpike road was put through from Cincinnati to Brookville, Indiana, in 1838, this library was no longer located at a common meeting place, and was neglected.

About twenty years later a second subscription for a library followed renewed interest in the community, and at present the library is actively functioning.

WILLIAM BEBB AND HIS SCHOOL

William Bebb, oldest child of Edward Bebb and Margaret, his wife, was born in a frontier settlement in a frontier state, from foreign-born parents who were seeking a livelihood and independence not possible in their native land. There were three Bebb children.

All the opportunities locally possible were given them. Very probably the first book teaching was done by the mother, but you may be sure that after the age of 6 or 8 William Bebb had at least three or four months of schooling every year. We have his own appreciative evidence as to the skill and information of David Lloyd and his unfavorable comments on an earlier teacher. All the Bebb line have exceptional memories, as well as ability to learn by observation and to apply that knowledge with good judgment.

Naturally William and his brother worked on the home farm and neither ever lost his interest in things agricultural. During school sessions they had regular chores, night and morning, for which they were held responsible.

We can infer that William Bebb was a fine student. He was examined for his certificate by James Shields, the Glasgow graduate, and began teaching the Paddy's Run district in 1826. His next school was at North Bend, the home of General W. H. Harrison. Shortly after his marriage in 1828, and possibly influenced by the Thomas boarding school started in Paddy's Run some years before, young Bebb started a boarding school for boys from 10 to 14 years old on the family farm. It was a success from the start. There is nothing except the story of Robert Owen's New Harmony project going on about this same time in Indiana that is as spectacular as the few bits of information I have been able to gather about this Sycamore Grove School on Dry Fork.

If I knew all the high points of ultra-modern education I think I could show that Bebb had foreshadowed many, if not most, of them in his methods. The development of interest and of groups of related interests, as well as the project method with its plan, assembly, and completion, are perfectly evident.

The freedom of the frontier encouraged direct attack on problems rather than following traditional methods. Moreover, a strong, healthy helpmeet with a genius for cooking and for handling boys was an asset which cannot be disregarded. I have been able to find no facts as to the curriculum or tuition charged per term, but a letter describing the Bebb school in the Cincinnati Enquirer of September 14, 1879, by Judge A. W. C. Carter, who spent two years in the school, is much more interesting.

The school house, which faced east, was just across the road west of the Dry Fork. The central part held the school rooms, the south wing was the boys' dormitory, and Mr. Bebb and his family lived in the north wing. There were from 30 to 40 boarders from Cincinnati and the South and a few local day pupils.

The year was divided into two five-month terms, with a month's vacation between each two terms. School hours each day were from 9 to 12 and from 2 to 5. The assembly room was 20 feet by 30 feet with rows of desks for the students on three sides and the teacher's desk on the fourth. In spite of the large wood stove in the center of this room and the fireplace in the dining room, it was cold in the winter. According to Judge Carter, there was no way of heating the dormitory and as the whole building stood on piers, chilblains and frosted feet were the usual thing. There were no washing facilities in the dormitory and any face or hand washing was done at the creek just over the road.

The boys were encouraged to build cabins of their own and given the privilege of cutting logs from the woods along the stream. The more pretentious of these log cabins were two-room affairs with stone fireplaces and brick chimneys and during the winter they were probably more comfortable than the frame dormitory. The boys were permitted to be in the cabins in the evening, but they had to be back in the dormitory at Mr. Bebb's inspection hour in the morning. It must have been an ideal life after the homesick period had passed. Skating, swimming, and fishing came in their seasons. The boys learned to cook sunfish, catfish, chubs, suckers, goggle-eyes (rock bass), soft-shelled turtles, snappers, and crayfish in their fireplaces.

The orchards of the venerable "Uncle" or "Sir" (Edward Bebb) were free to the boys when the fruit was ripe as long as they did not club the fruit out of the trees. Groups of two boys, as partners, were assigned plots of ground by William Bebb; on these they raised what they liked best to eat. Probably there was some private agreements arrived at among the groups as to the diversification of food, and certainly there were few insect parasites to be fed then as compared to the present.

Mr. Bebb was justice of the peace and legal adviser for most of the inhabitants of Morgan Township. Civil and criminal court cases were held in the assembly room with the boys (10 to 14 years old) all required to be present at their desks during the trials. No wonder many of his pupils grew up to become lawyers, judges, and political leaders.

About this time there was a period when military training for men came into fashion. According to Judge Carter, "Mr. Bebb was a militia commander and when in his regimentals, mounted on his black stallion on his way to the parade grounds, he was a sight to us boys indeed."

Among the students who attended the Sycamore Grove School, in addition to Judge Carter, whose article is the source of my information, were the following:

William Dennison, Governor of Ohio, 1859-61.

Charles Larrabee, born in Rome, New York, 1820. (His father was a Major in the U. S. Army and by appointment of President Jackson, 1828-36, was surveyor of the Port of Cincinnati.) After the Bebb school closed in 1832 he attended an academy in Springfield and later Granville College (now Denison University). At 24 he went to Chicago to practice law. In 1847 he moved to Wisconsin, where he lived for nearly twenty years. He was a member of the second Constitutional Convention of Wisconsin; was a circuit judge for ten years;

was a Representative in Washington, 1858-60; and served in the Union Army as Captain, Major and Colonel, 1861-63, retiring because of ill health. For the sake of his health he moved to the west. He became a member of the first Constitutional Convention of Washington Territory. Later he made his home near San Bernardino, California, practicing law and breeding new plants and fruits. He lost his life in a railroad accident, January 20, 1883.

Dr. G. M. Shaw, of Indiana.

Daniel Shaw, sheriff of Grant Parish, member of the Louisiana Legislature.

Peter Melendy, of Iowa, who was active in establishing Iowa State College at Ames.

Hampton Davis, mayor of Vicksburg, Mississippi.

Augustus Jordan, prominent lawyer in New Orleans.

When in 1832 Mr. Bebb gave up Sycamore Grove and moved to Hamilton to take up the practice of law, the whole of Butler and Hamilton counties and neighboring Indiana regretted the loss of the school.

HAMILTON, 1832-1850

Mr. Bebb, already well known in Hamilton, as he had been one of the county teachers' examiners for years, developed a good law practice there, but he did not lose his interest in teaching. In 1835 he drafted a bill to charter a female academy in Hamilton and became an adviser to the management.

He was interested in all public movements, and was an ardent advocate of the educational value of county fairs for farmers and spoke for them at other county seats.

At the Buckeye Celebration, September 30, 1835, in honor of the completion of Fort Hamilton by General St. Clair forty-four years previously, Mr. Bebb was the orator of the day. He emphasized the merits of the Ordinance of 1787, and especially commended the exclusion of involuntary servitude from the Northwest Territory. He said: "We meddle not with slavery as it exists in the South. Only one catastrophe can arrest the onward career of the country, and that is a severance of the union." So it is clear that both these questions were in the air at the time.

He took an active part in politics as a Whig and campaigned

for William Henry Harrison in both 1836 and 1840. The election of Polk in 1844 settled both the admission of Texas in 1845 and the certainty of war with Mexico.

In 1846 Bebb was elected governor of Ohio, the third governor born in the state and the first from the southwestern part of the state. The Mexican war was unpopular with the northern Whigs because of the increase of slave territory. Elected governor by a party unfavorable to the war, and being himself against it, he nevertheless fell into line, believing that the loyal support of the government was more important than consistency to a party.

The State House in Columbus had been authorized seven years earlier, but for some reason nothing had been done. Bebb sent a message to the Legislature dealing chiefly with the construction of the State House, and though it was not completed for six more years, his prodding produced visible results. Ohio was prosperous during his term of office, showing good money, advances in schools, activity in the construction of railroads and turnpikes, and good business conditions generally.

In his final message, printed in 1849, he said that the majority in the United States was against the extension of slavery into New Mexico and California, and that any compromise passed by Congress against the will of the majority would "cause the lightning to burst forth hereafter with more terrific and astounding effect."

His little daughter, Sarah, died of acute appendicitis (as we would call it now) in 1848, and was buried in Greenwood Cemetery which had been obtained for Hamilton in great part through his efforts.

Discouraged by the national prospects, he decided to retire from the law. He purchased a large tract of land on Rock River in Illinois and in 1850 moved there, traveling via the Miami and Erie canal to Toledo and by lake boat from there around to Chicago. With his household goods he took the coffin of his daughter from Greenwood, and she was re-buried in Illinois.

As the slavery question became more and more serious many former Whigs turned Abolitionist. The Whig party and Henry

Clay believed in compromise, or appeasement as we call it today, and I think Governor Bebb went to his parents' old home in Wales in 1855 and arranged for a new Welsh colony to the United States with some such object in mind as demonstrating the greater efficiency of free over slave labor. In this colony were two of his own first cousins, Samuel and George Roberts. There is no reason why he should have chosen East Tennessee instead of Illinois, Iowa, or even Wisconsin, for the location of the colony unless he hoped that the example to be set by the 100 industrious free Welsh he was helping to emigrate would tend gradually to educate the South away from slavery.

In May, 1857, his son, Michael, married and went to the Illinois home on his wedding trip. A number of the hoodlums of the neighborhood arranged an evening charivari or "belling," bringing guns and bells and flasks. Mr. Bebb ordered them off to no avail. They were too full of their artificial courage to be frightened away by firing over their heads. He fired again at a lower level and killed one of the roisterers.

He was tried for manslaughter in the Rockford County Court. It was a notable case. Two of his former coadjutors in Ohio courts, Ex-Governor Tom Corwin of Lebanon, and Judge W. T. Johnston of Cincinnati, volunteered to assist his Rockford attorneys for old friendship's sake. The trial lasted four days and the jury after deliberating for four hours brought in a verdict of not guilty. The notes of Governor Corwin's speech were filed with the official papers for their wonderful oratory and convincing argument.

As the Welsh colony in Tennessee needed superintending and legal guidance, the family moved there, and Mr. Bebb began the practice of law in Knoxville. His son, Edward, drove 200 sheep from Rockford, Illinois, to Huntsville, Tennessee, between December 19, 1857, and January 10, 1858, during which time they were "snowed up" once in Indiana.

In January, 1860, Mr. Bebb wrote his sister in Paddy's Run: "We have been received with marked attention and friendship by the people of Knoxville. Nine-tenths of them are old Whigs of the Henry Clay school. I apprehended that we might find trouble in the present excited state of public opinion but I have not seen or heard anything unkind toward the people of the North."

However, in a letter from Knoxville six months later, Mr. Bebb, after speaking of the railroad he had hoped to encourage the business men of Cincinnati to start (the present Cincinnati Southern) and telling of half a dozen law cases he had conducted in Knoxville and vicinity, said that he hoped to devote the rest of his life to his profession *which he should never have quit* (italics his). He then said to his sister: "The more I see of slavery the less I like it. Not because the slaves are not well treated, but because of its general influence upon the whites and upon the industrial and moral trend of society. We have an excellent house, much like our Hamilton house, and a good garden. We have one good colored girl whom we hire at $6.00 per month."

Mr. Bebb made a few speeches in Illinois that summer in favor of Lincoln and word was sent him that he had better not come back to Tennessee. His Welsh colony also scattered over the northern United States after the beginning of the Civil War. After his family left their Tennessee home it was broken into and looted by Southern sympathizers. His portrait was slashed with a saber. Later some of his possessions were reclaimed and sent to Washington, where he was employed as Patent Office examiner from 1861 to 1869. The damaged portrait is still in Washington, the property of one of his grandsons.

At home in Rockford he took pneumonia following exposure undergone when returning from making a speech in favor of General U. S. Grant for President. It was his first serious illness, but he never fully recovered. He died in Rockford October 23, 1873.

His son, Michael Schuck Bebb, was a well known amateur botanist and correspondent of Asa Gray of Harvard. His brother, Evan Bebb, became a business man in New York City. The firm of Bebb and Graham preceded the pioneer department store of A. T. Stewart and Company.

Other Nationally Known Men

The Paddy's Run community did not stop when it produced a native-born Governor of Ohio.

Governor James Brown Ray of Indiana, born in Jefferson County, Kentucky, 1794, attended school in Paddy's Run, probably living across the line in Franklin County, Indiana. He studied law in Cincinnati. He was the last non-partisan governor elected anywhere in the United States as far as I know. He advocated railroads running like spokes of a wheel out from Indianapolis. He served from 1825 to 1831. He died of cholera in Cincinnati in 1848.

A number of noted ministers have close connection with Paddy's Run. The Rev. Benjamin W. Chidlaw, born in Wales, graduate of the class of 1833 of Miami University, began his preaching there and then spent fifty years in the service of the Sunday School Union.

Dr. Thomas Ebenezer Thomas was graduated from Miami in 1834. He was a member of the first anti-slavery group in Butler County, and became a well known Abolitionist. He was for some years president of Hanover College in Indiana, and then was a professor in the New Albany Theological Seminary. When this school was moved to Chicago as McCormick Seminary, Dr. Thomas was dropped with others because of their radical views on slavery. He was a moderator of a Presbyterian General Assembly and died in harness while teaching at Lane Theological Seminary in Cincinnati.

Dr. Mark Williams, Miami '58, was a missionary to North China for 54 years, having been sent out when the route to China was by sailing vessel eastward around the Cape of Good Hope instead of westward across the Pacific by steamer.

Among writers, Paddy's Run has made notable contribution in the persons of Murat Halstead and Albert Shaw.

Murat Halstead, from whom I quoted the description of the valley, was a student at Farmer's College, a war correspondent in the Franco-Prussian and Spanish-American Wars, editor of the Cincinnati Commercial for many years, editor of the Brooklyn Graphic, and author of books on Cuba and the Philippines.

Albert Shaw, son of Dr. Griffin and Susan Fisher Shaw, now 88 years old, is a graduate of Grinnell College, Iowa. He received a Ph.D. degree from Johns Hopkins University in 1884. Editor of the Minneapolis Tribune from 1883-1890, except for a year during which he studied in Europe, Dr. Shaw established the Review of Reviews in 1891, editing it until his retirement in 1937. A life senator of Phi Beta Kappa, he is the author of eleven books in the field of government and political science. Seven universities have given him the honorary degree of LL.D. and four the Litt.D. degree, among them Miami University in 1929.

I will end with the mention of two brothers, descendants of David and Mary Francis, of the group of passengers on the Maria in 1795, who are also grandnephews of Governor Bebb.

Dr. Mark Francis, Ohio State University, 1887, was for many years a professor of veterinary medicine in Texas A. and M. College. He devised a method of immunizing cattle against the tick fever and so made possible the development of the great cattle industry of the Southwest.

President William Oxley Thompson of Ohio State, speaking about 1915, said of Dr. Francis, the first graduate of the Ohio State University School of Veterinary Medicine, that if that University during the forty-odd years of its existence had done nothing but give Mark Francis to the world, it would have earned all it had cost to the state of Ohio up to that time.

Dr. Edward Francis, Ohio State University, 1894, public health surgeon, is retired, but still at work in a government laboratory in Washington. He is known among his colleagues as the human test tube, because he has suffered from many of the diseases with which he has worked. He is best known for his studies of tularemia or rabbit fever, on which he has had numerous publications since 1919. Rocky Mountain spotted fever, undulant fever, and tick or relapsing fever are other diseases his work has helped scientists to understand.

I am sad to have to report that centralization of the public schools and mail from Hamilton by rural free delivery may leave nothing of the village on the Paddy's Run, which has produced more than 250 college graduates, but the crossroads. However, the stock, whether Welsh, early American, or German, is still surviving, scattered over our forty-eight states, and should continue to give a good account of itself.

CHAPTER II

EARLY DAYS

THE WILD ANIMALS

NONE of the white settlers who came to the area of the Great Miami in 1800 ever saw a wild buffalo. Although these were known by the colonists in the Atlantic states, they were never abundant because of the few prairie openings. These beasts made paths along the hill tops as they migrated in search of food and the Indian file of the warpath followed these paths. The last record of a buffalo killed in Ohio seems to be in the Hocking Valley in 1794. By 1820 there were few, if any, east of the Mississippi.

The last bear killed near Paddy's Run was in 1809, in Section 6, four miles north of the village; the last in the county, 1833, was in Fairfield Township.

A large panther was killed near the line between Reily and Morgan Townships in 1815. In an old township book of about that time there are records of several cases of payment for wolf scalps.

Andrew Lewis reported that soon after 1800 he saw, on his way to Millville, fourteen deer, all broadside on and easy shots, but he needed no venison. According to the county history, the last deer taken in the county was killed at Stilwell's Corner, two townships north, in 1825.

Mr. Chidlaw's reference in Appendix III to the James child killed in 1800 by a rattlesnake bite is all that has been found on poisonous snakes. A community which so early began to raise hogs in quantity, and had so few rocky shelters, would likely have lost such reptiles early and without knowing it. There were, no doubt, both rattlesnakes and copperheads, but never in abundance.

Wild turkeys, which could be trapped in log pens, were numerous in the early days of the settlement. Over 100 were chased out of one cornfield in which they were feeding.

Passenger pigeons, during migration, could be shot without aiming.

The level land of Oxford, Reily, and Morgan Townships was swampy and dotted with ponds and here in spring and fall migrating water fowl abounded.

The Cincinnati Gazette of 1828 ran a regular advertisement, "We wish to purchase Wildcat, Fox, Mink, Otter, Raccoon and Rabbit Skins."

To give an idea of what the supply of wild life must have been in all this area, Cist's Miscellany, Vol. 2, gives a long list brought in from Randolph and Jay counties, Indiana, in three months, December, January, and February, 1846, by one hunter and sold on the Cincinnati market. This is only part of the list:

74 whole deer, 270 deer saddles at 4 to 5 cents a pound;
4,300 rabbits, 10-12 cents apiece;
2,290 pheasants, $1.50-$2.00 per dozen (Ruffed Grouse);
10,000 quail, 60-75 cents a dozen;
90 wild turkeys, 75 cents each.

Forty years previously the same abundance would have held in southwestern Ohio.

The multitude of passenger pigeons decreased suddenly in 1852. In 1885 there were still scattered flights of few birds, and shortly thereafter when the pine woods of Michigan, where the birds habitually nested, were cut, the bird became extinct.

About this time clearing of the rougher parts of farms for the lumber reduced the number of foxes and, conversely, the groundhog and rabbit became commoner.

Wolves from the north may still appear here in their search for food in severe winters. In 1933 one was crippled by a gunshot as it was taking a pig from the Eschenbrenners' barnyard on Paddy's Run. This wolf, with a hind foot shot away, was able to exist for almost two years, ranging from the boundary of Hamilton County along Paddy and off into the hills of Ross Township. At last his lair was located and a gunner lying in wait shot him from a distance.

The most dangerous of the animals inhabiting this region when the white man came to it was, without a doubt, the

EARLY DAYS

malarial mosquito. In the early days the "shakes" or fever and ague were the rule rather than the exception. Ditching fields and draining low spots removed the breeding places and quinine cured the disease.

When a boy I had malaria two summers in succession. It was cured by quinine after frost removed the danger of reinfection. The second winter a hickory flats woods, a quarter of a mile southwest of the house was cleared and ditched and my malaria was a thing of the past. Now that there are no malarial patients the uninfected mosquitoes merely bite us.

Contacts With the Indians

Since the land was not surveyed and put on sale until 1801, six years after Wayne's treaty at Greenville, the early settlers in Morgan Township were not molested by Indians. Mr. Chidlaw (Appendix III, page 179), in discussing the Bebb clock, indicates that Indians were not uncommon, however.

At one time fourteen braves, possibly Wyandots (Iroquois) came to Edward Bebb's house on Dry Fork, laid their guns down by the sycamore at the gate, struck their tomahawks into the tree and hung their powder horns and bullet pouches on the handles, all as a sign of peaceful intent. Coming up to the house the spokesman asked for food. The table was loaded with a generous supply of whatever edibles were available. The men put salt by handfuls on everything they ate, even on the pickled pork out of the brine. When they had eaten all they could hold, they gathered up the food remaining on the table and took it with them.

Long after the removal of the Indian tribes from this region an old man came back to revisit the scenes of his younger days. Coming to Bebb's he asked, "Where my friend the white man? Dead?"

"Oh, no," Mrs. Bebb responded, "Mr. Bebb is working up on the hill and will be down soon."

The Indian grunted, "Mebbe so, mebbe lie, me don't know." He stayed over night and the boys (the future Governor, William Bebb, and his brother, Evan) got him to dance the war-dance in the sitting room before the fire. A man, whose name was likewise William Bebb, and his wife, freshly arrived from Wales, were occupying the bedroom opening off from this sitting room. They went to bed early, taking the ax from the woodshed with them and as the old warrior danced with his "Yo-hi, yo-hi yea—yo-hi, yo-hi, yaw, yea," stamping on the floor and leaping into the air about as high as the table, I suspect that the recent immigrants were clutching the ax handle inside the bedroom door.

Howe's History of Ohio says that the oldest church building in Morgan Township was located two miles south of the Bebbs' and three miles north of New Haven on the Butler-Hamilton county line. The church was of round logs. Its burying ground was in the lower ground toward Dry Fork. There were about fifty interments there before it was abandoned in 1827. This is almost certainly the place of burial of Adam Poe, an Indian fighter best known for his battle with the Indian, Big Foot.

The owner of the farm in 1940 told me that in plowing the field containing the cemetery, he can both feel and hear differences as the plow crosses an old grave, in spite of the century and more which has passed since a burial there.

The John Evans spring with the James Shields house in the background. The Robinson hewed log house (the Rev. Thomas' schoolhouse) (see pages 146-150). Soap making, the ash hopper is behind the kettles.

The 1852-56 Congregational church. The first church, 1825, now remodeled, the community house. The Catholic church. The fourth schoolhouse, 1852. The present Congregational church. The 1872 school building, now the home of the Shandon library.

CHAPTER III

IMPLEMENTS, HOUSE AND FARM

ALL COOKING was done in the fireplaces as there were no cookstoves in the early 1800's. Iron pots and kettles were swung on the crane over the fire, and Dutch ovens were set before the fire, their contents to cook by radiant heat. Skillets were used for frying over a bed of coals drawn forward from the main fire; baking was done in hot ashes. When corn is in the milk and may be cooked in its husk in ashes we still call it roasting ears. Ripe corn, parched in the skillet, was also enjoyed by the early settlers.

Fire light, lard oil lamps and tallow candles were used. Fires were carefully tended as there were no matches. A skillful person could kindle "punk" wood by snapping his gunflint as though to discharge the gun. There also were large perforated shovels to be used in carrying a blazing chunk from a neighbor's if the distance to be covered was not too great.

Knives were comparatively few and one invited out to a meal was expected to bring his own. When forks were first made they had but two tines and were ineffective as far as small objects such as peas or beans were concerned. The first table knives had an enormous enlargement at the back of the tip, which made an instrument with which peas and other small things could readily be shoveled into the mouth. Anything liquid enough to drink was so treated.

Spoons were of wood or horn unless the settlers had brought pewter or silver from the old country.

Before the white settlers came, the Indians ground their cornmeal by using a stone pestle and a burned-out hardwood stump. As soon as water power to turn millstones could be utilized it replaced the hand mill as more rapid and efficient.

My great-grandmother used a rawhide sieve with numerous nailholes punched through the dry hide for sifting cornmeal. For wheat flour she had a smaller frame with black horse hairs woven across the bottom. I do not remember how the hairs were fastened to the wooden frame.

The primitive fork for handling barley, rye, or wheat was a three-pronged wooden one. In later years this was used as a chaff fork. Rakes were much like the present all-wood rake —if you can find one.

Sickles were used for cutting the grain and scythes for hay. After being bound, the sheaves were shocked as now, but were stored in barns for flailing out the grain in the winter. One man could not harvest more than ten acres of grain a year because of the limitation of space to store and time to flail. Even then he would have to enlist help as he winnowed the seed which had to be poured from some height in front of a flapping sheet. I doubt if a husk more or less troubled him.

Some genius developed a light carrier to be fastened to his scythe so that standing wheat, when cut by the blade, would fall gently into the cradle, as this combination was named. By a few careful swings he could have a sheaf ready for binding. Later a mower for hay was given the same sort of a device to cut and carry and drop a sheaf so that one man and team could cut and drop the sheaves as fast as eight or ten men could bind them. This was replaced by the self-binder and then by the combine, the last word in mechanical harvesting, which does all in one process what was once done from sickle in July to flail and winnowing sheet in February.

Every man among the early settlers was what would be called in these days a skilled ax-man. With his ax, an auger and a frow he could build a home. Given a dozen good men, a sturdy one-room cabin could be erected in two days from the time of starting to cut the first tree. This time would not include a cat and clay chimney or a puncheon floor, but these were luxuries to the early woodsmen. They did not need iron. Even in the David Francis barn, built after 1812, the frame was all pegged and the planks of the driveway pinned to the hewed floor joists. The siding may have been nailed; if so, hand-made nails from the local blacksmith's were used.

Soap Day

The early settlers on Paddy's Run were their own soap-makers. In the fall the ash-hopper would be cleaned out and

IMPLEMENTS, HOUSE AND FARM

the ashes from the fireplace and wood stove stored there during the winter. In the early spring when hard freezing was a thing of the past, water was poured over these ashes daily, the liquid appearing at the the lower end of the foundation, a hollowed-out log, as (potash) lye. When this lye became so sufficiently concentrated that it could float an egg, the hambones and skins and fat which had been accumulated from the winter's meat were brought out of the cellar and set to boiling with the lye in iron kettles. When a kettle threatened to boil over it was treated with a ladle of cold lye.

The result of this cooking was brown soft soap, which was stored in a barrel in the cellar. At the very last of the soap-making, a kettle of grease was treated with lye bought at the store in a can (soda lye). This resulted in a grayish white hard soap, which when cooled and cut, was dried on the attic floor and used as hand soap.

THE BLACKSMITH SHOP

The blacksmith shop was an interesting place. The man within had to be an adaptable mechanic. There were no drives to collect scrap-iron in the 1800's. Every bit was cherished and used. Nails could be made as you watched and so could horseshoes. That was a tedious task, because after the shoe had been roughed out from a bar of iron it had to be fitted carefully to the horse's foot. It took many tries and much trimming of the hoof where the hot shoe seared it before the satisfied smith reached for his nail box which had been sitting some distance away in safety through all the preliminaries. Taking a horse to be shod all around was a task, especially in the summer, when it was the duty of the boy who took the horse to protect with a horse-tail flybrush the leg opposite to the one the smith was busy with.

Setting the tires on wheels was not a waiting job. After driving through the creek and soaking up the spokes and fellies (rim) ceased to be sufficient, the tire had to be reset finally and the conveyance was taken to the shop and left there. When he had leisure, the blacksmith would run a small measuring wheel inside the tire he had removed from its wheel and find out how much and where to cut the tire. When it had been welded again and by measure was the correct size, he would lay it flat, set a pile of chips and wood on it so as to make a circular, hot fire covering the tire. The wooden part of the wheel was set flat in such a way that it rested on the rim. Then, using tongs, the smith placed the tire, red-hot all the way around, over the rim and he and his assistant gently drove it into place, wet it to prevent damaging the rim and as it cooled it became firmer and firmer. Hence the term "set the tire."

The blacksmith was really the village repairer. Anything made of wood was replaceable at home, but whatever involved metal was beyond household tools and had to go to the smith.

CHAPTER IV

1818 IMMIGRANTS AND MORGAN GWILYM'S LETTER TO WALES

AFTER the first Welsh settled the Paddy's Run valley, it took time for the good news to filter back to the old country. Then as the War of 1812 prevented all immigration, it was not until 1818 (see Appendix III) that a large group came. Most of these were from Montgomeryshire. Their ship missed the Delaware River, and instead came up the Chesapeake Bay, landing the strangers at Alexandria, Virginia. To do honor to this large addition to the population of their country, President Monroe and his cabinet went down to the dock to greet these future citizens.

In contrast to this reception, when the migrants reached Cincinnati, no hotel or boarding house in that small place would receive them because of cases of dysentery aboard the boat on which they had come down the river. Nicholas Longworth took the whole party to his own home and cared for them while they were making connection with their friends at Paddy's Run.

Two brothers, John and William B. Davis, sons of William Davis and Ann Jones, both of this group, became leading physicians in Cincinnati. Both were on the faculty of the Miami Medical College, now a part of the present College of Medicine of the University of Cincinnati.

The following letter from Morgan Gwilym, one of the passengers on the Maria from Bristol in 1795, to his brother in Wales after the lapse of twenty-three years, shows his full appreciation of the country of his adoption and his desire for others to share in his good fortune:

"Dear Brother: We Rec'd. your letter Dated February 20th, 1817, sometime in the month of October and was very glad to hear that you my brother John was well and in tolerable good circumstances.

"I was very sorry to hear that my native country is in such a deplorable situation when we here enjoy peace and plenty. Mr. Evan Jones and his brother-in-law Evan Davies and family arrived safe here some time in the fall in good health. Evan Davies has purchased him 80 acres of land and has paid for it about 2 Miles from us.

"I understood from him that you had some notions of coming to our happy land which gave me some faint hope of seeing you once more. I suppose as the time is hard there that perhaps you would have to sell your stock low. If any of your rich knaibors was coming over and you having too little to bring you over I shall be very happy to repay them their money here, but hoping that the time will alter for the better and you to have good price for your stock etc.

"You wanted to know whether I was married or not. I suppose Evan Jones has told you our circumstances but for fear he has not I shall give you a full acct. I have lived good part of my time in the State of Pennsylvania and about ten years ago got married to a Welsh girl from the County of Montgomery, North Wales.

"I have four daughters, the eldest Eliza 9 years old and Rachel about 7 years and 9 months, third Nancy about 5 years, fourth Hannah 2 years old. We have done very well in this country. Have a fine farm which would sell for about 6000 Dollars and every other thing in proportion. William has done tolerable well too. As he has sent you a letter I shall not say anything concerning.

"Hugh and John Rees live in the State of Pennsylvania and is doing tolerable well, have good many children, married. Wm. Harry and Watkin Rees Bowen are both dead. Will or Garryd has lived here for some time and about ten years left here for Wales and we never heard from him since.

"We have places of worship here among us but I have not joined with any of them as yet but allways live according to the good old rule do as you would be done by. There are Presbyterians, Babtists, Covenanters, Methodists (Wesley), few Universalists, Unitarians, etc.

"I shall give you the price of things here—Good waggin Horse from seventy to Hundred Dollars. Milch cow from 16 to 24 dollars. Beef from four to five dollars Hd., pork about the same. Wheat three quarter Dollars bushel. Rye half dollar. Indian corn about the same. Flax ⅛ dollar per lb. Potatoes 3 bushels for one dollar. The dollar is 4s 6d of your money. For instant wheat 3s 4½d per bushel. Days labour half dollar per day and found or a bushel of wheat and find themselfs. Mechanics gets . . . Blacksmiths about dollar and fifty cents, Carpenters masons, etc. the same.

"Who would stay in your tiranical country? We here choose our own Judges every seven years, Justices of the Peace every three years. Every one has a vote in choosing all our offices from the president of the United States to the constable.

"Every one worships Almighty God according to the dicktates of his own Conscience, thank God no orthodoxy no tithes no high church no king but good and wholesome laws. If you or any of you will come over I shall do a good part for you for thank God we have plenty. Give our best love to William Lewis and my dear sister and all our inquiring friends. Send a letter and let know your welfare. No more at present but remain your dear Brother til death."

(Signed) Morgan Gwillum

The letter was addressed: John Gwillum Languke to be left at Neath postoffice Glamorganshire, South Wales, Great Britain, to be left to the care of Thomas Arthur Ironmonger.

CHAPTER V

A SQUIRREL HUNT IN SOUTHWESTERN BUTLER COUNTY IN 1828

Written for the Hamilton Democrat by Flora B. Shields, granddaughter of James Shields who issued the call for the hunt. Date of article Nov. 26, 1903.

"Notice of Squirrel Hunt."

"We, the undersigned inhabitants of the southeast part of Morgan Township and southwest part of Ross, in Butler County and the north edge of Crosby Township, Hamilton County, considering the importance of destroying the squirrels which abound in our neighborhood, promise to pay cash, the quantity of corn given opposite our names, to be distributed in prizes to the persons who shall kill the greatest, next greatest, &c, numbers of squirrels on Monday and Tuesday of the present month, April, 1828, on which day it is intended to have a Squirrel hunt.

"The following is to be a part of the condition: The hunters are to hunt only around the fields of each person who will subscribe. And on Tuesday evening, the 22nd, the scalps are to be brought to some place most central. He who has the greatest number of scalps shall have the largest prize (the number of prizes will be five). Every person shall be upon his honor that he has killed on these two days the squirrels of whose scalps he may bring forward; he may have as many drivers as he pleases; but no squirrel may be shot but by himself. This subscription paper shall be brought to the count of scalps, and each winner shall receive orders for the amount of corn which the judges, who shall then be chosen, shall award. If any one hunts out of the boundaries or has any one to shoot for him he forfeits all prizes. Crows and hawks and owls count as two squirrels."

Subscribers' Names	Bu. Corn
John Mering	3
James Shields	3
Dan'l Bottenberg	3
James Nicholas	3
Morgan Gwilym	3
James Nicholas, Jr.	3
Abner Francis	2
Nicholas Anderson	1
Maurice Jones	3
Martin Vertz	1
William Vaughn	3
Daniel Vaughn	2
Evan Morris	3
John Burch	2
Richard Richard	1
James Broun	3
Richard Jones	1
Griffith Breece	2
Martin Beessear (Busseur)	3
John Evans	2
Hiram Hall	2
—— Cronkhill	1
John Whitehead	2
Col. Griffin Halstead	3
V. Guerin	3

Amount of corn subscribed, 54 bushels, to be divided into prizes, as follows:

1st prize, one-third of the whole number	18 bushels
2nd prize, one-third of the remainder	12 bushels
3rd prize, one-third of the remainder	8 bushels
4th prize	8 bushels
5th prize	8 bushels

The Result

Col. Griffin Halstead produced 105 squirrel scalps and 2 owls	109
Dan'l Bottenberg produced 137 squirrel scalps and 6 owls	149
James Nicholas, Jr. produced 119 squirrel scalps	119
Capt. Abner Francis produced 113 squirrel scalps	113
John Mering produced 113 squirrel scalps and one owl	115
Thomas J. Shields produced 166 squirrel scalps	166
John Burch produced 108 squirrel scalps	108

Prize Winners

Thomas J. Shields, first prize, 166 squirrels, 18 bushels corn
Dan'l Bottenberg, second prize, 149 squirrels, 12 bushels corn
James Nicholas, Jr., third prize, 119 squirrels, 8 bushels corn
John Mering, fourth prize, 115 squirrels, 8 bushels corn
Abner Francis, fifth prize, 113 squirrels, 8 bushels corn

The area covered by this most successful hunting covered in Morgan Township all of sections 25 and 36, possibly parts of 26 and 35; in Ross Township part of section 19, all of section 30 and much of 31; in Crosby Township, Hamilton County, the area is undeterminable but not large. All told there might have been six square miles or more. If no shot missed, the hunters charged their muzzle-loading rifles at least eight hundred and sixty times in the two days. In view of the necessity of having the scalps to turn in, I assume those who hunted were careful to aim at the lower edge of the eye, which, I understand, is the correct target of a real squirrel hunter.

Audubon writes of seeing squirrels in hordes swimming the Ohio River at Henderson, Kentucky. Evidently the white man's universal culture of Indian corn stimulated the squirrel population much as the transfer from Europe has increased the numbers of the "English sparrow" or, in more recent years, the starling.

CHAPTER VI

THE MIGRATION TO GOMER, 1833

THE LAND purchase of Ezekiel Hughes and Edward Bebb in 1801 as soon as land west of the Miami River was on the market, was the start of an active Welsh immigration, especially from Montgomeryshire into Ohio. The small valley of the Paddy's Run was filled and later comers spread out over the surrounding hills.

About 1820 the Indians were bargained out of the northwest corner of the state, solemnly reserved for them by the treaty of Greenville, and by 1832 the whole Black Swamp region was opened for settlement. In 1833 Thomas Watkins, David Roberts, James Nicholas Jr., and their immediate families drove from Paddy's Run up to the present Gomer, Allen County, where they had purchased land in Sugar Creek Township. The distance was about 130 miles.

At that time the roads as far as Piqua, where the land office was located and the deeds obtained, had been improved to some extent, but it is likely bridges were few and fords were the usual pathways across the streams. The Miami and Erie Canal had been completed as far as Dayton and it may be assumed that a caravan of loaded wagons, burdened with two cows, the property of Thomas Watkins, followed the most level pathway.

I have discovered nothing concerning the separate stages of this journey. It was evidently intentionally planned for the early autumn, the driest part of the year. There were trails of a sort beyond Piqua on the former Indian reservation, but no bridges. Dense forest lined each side of the track. Some of that country is swampy and many brush-filled mud holes and sections of "corduroy road" had to be traversed in the low ground. At the rate of twenty miles a day the travelers would have camped near the present cities of Middletown, Dayton, Troy, Sidney, Wapakoneta and perhaps Lima on their way. We know that they arrived in Gomer on September 13, 1833, and it may be that they started about the first of September and traveled at a much slower pace than I have suggested.

There is no mention of other men besides the heads of the three families in the group, so the three men, with help from their wives, must have built their log cabins, one after the other. In three weeks the Watkins' cabin, a one-room affair with a door-opening and oiled paper over a window, was occupied. As there was no grass for the cows in the forest, they browsed on the underbrush and on the leaves of the tops of the trees from which the logs were cut. The other two houses were completed before winter.

According to David Nicholas, the youngest son of Squire and Mrs. Nicholas, soon after arriving in this wilderness, and before the Nicholas cabin was provided with a door, Mr. Nicholas had to be away from home. Mrs. Nicholas took her baby daughter, Jane, climbed up on the joists in the cabin, and spent the night there to avoid the wolves that howled nearby. These were the times and the places where the story of Red Ridinghood had not yet faded into a fairy tale.

The nearest point of supply for the group was Sandusky, 80 miles to the northeast, and the round trip for a lightly-loaded two-horse wagon took six days. At that time it took a wagon-load of corn to buy a barrel of salt.

Fifteen years later, under the auspices of Governor Bebb, three other men, William Bebb (Rhiwgriafol), Thomas Morris, Richard Jarvis and their families from Paddy's Run founded the Welsh settlement of Venedocia, west of Gomer in Van Wert County.

CHAPTER VII

EARTHQUAKES AND METEORITES

THE 1811-12 EARTHQUAKES

STARTING December 16, 1811, a number of earthquake shocks were felt violently throughout the Paddy's Run neighborhood. Some were severe enough to crack ice on the creeks and to break icicles off the trees.

Mrs. Mary Bebb Vaughan relates that on one occasion (she was then only six years old) she was playing on the ice when a shock of earthquake came, throwing her prostrate. With difficulty she succeeded in crawling over the cracked and shattered ice to the land.

Daniel Drake, in his "Picturesque Cincinnati," gives the times of the most severe shocks. The first, on December 16, 1811, was at 2:30 a.m., lasting for seven minutes. The next serious one was January 23, 1812, at 9 a.m., lasting from four to five minutes.

On February 7, 1812, shocks came which surpassed all previous ones, more chimneys were thrown down, more vertigo and nausea produced than at any other time. This was known as the day of the big shocks. They began at 3:45 p.m. and this would be the most likely time for a small child to be out at play. The ground is said to have moved in waves from west to east, the atmosphere was darkened by dust and fog and there were light flashes, probably lightning.

THE 1833 METEORITES

From Paddy's Run Papers No. II

by Murat Halstead. Copyright 1895

(The 1833 shower of meteorites as remembered from his fourth year.)

One November night our astronomical observations came to a climax, and, though an unwilling, I became a wondering spectator.

Fancy looking upon all the stars rushing in a mad torrent from the tip of the dome of the sky and disappearing at the horizon. Consider an aurora borealis with rapids of sparks forming an all-embracing cataract of silver flame, or the majestical o'er-hanging firmament fretted with golden fires, to such an extent that zenith seemed to be the bell-muzzled mouth of a Roman candle spreading vast sheets of falling stars. That was what happened on the night that Edwin Booth was born.

That day my father had killed a "mess of young squirrels," fat as butter with hickory nuts, and they were, I am not ashamed to say, my favorite meat, and there was not due vigilance in guarding me that I might not bear testimony "not wisely but too well" of the succulence of the squirrels and the richness of the gravy. Fortunately I was ill at one o'clock in the morning and aroused my parents, who were diverted from my difficulties by the discovery that while our world seemed to be pretty steady all the rest of the worlds were on fire.

Recovering from the pangs of too much squirrel I was wrapped in a blanket, and the dazzling celestial show was in full blast. Indeed, when one was out of doors, there was nothing to see but stars recklessly and in strange silence tumbling "headlong, flaming" through ethereal space with "hideous ruin and combustion." I did not know that there was any liability that the world might come to an end, going off on a trot with the giddy constellations, and when I got sleepy, I ceased to be a spectator.

Other men of the community, on the way to Cincinnati by night with hogs to sell, also reported this rain of stars but without the skill which Editor Halstead developed in the next sixty years.

Meteorites, November, 1833

Written by John Green Vaughan of Odin, Ill., Nov. 22, 1899, for his sister, M. A. Francis

I do remember very distinctly the falling stars in 1833. I was nearly seven years old at the time. Father called us all up between 3 and 4 o'clock in the morning to see the sight. They all came from east and northeast, and as I remember them, they appeared larger than stars of the first magnitude, and were as close together as you ever saw the stars in the sky. They nearly all had tails, some of them long and very bright. They continued to fall till broad daylight.

The Howards, who lived on the hill west of Evan Morris's, claimed that they saw huge balls of fire, larger than a hogshead, rolling and bouncing down the sides of those hills, but I did not see anything like that, nor heard of any damage being done by them.

CHAPTER VIII

LOCAL OUTBREAK OF ASIATIC CHOLERA, 1834

AS YOU know, cholera is endemic in the warm parts of Asia and from there epidemics have spread over the rest of the world. In 1817 an epidemic reached throughout most of Asia and the continents of Africa and Europe, while the one starting in 1826 reached North America in 1832. It was brought from Dublin, Ireland, on the ship Carricks in June and was taken on to Montreal by emigrants from the Carricks on the steamboat Voyage. From there it made its way along the inland waterways to the Mississippi system and by the end of 1832 was a serious problem in New Orleans. Returning up the Mississippi in 1833, it devastated Louisville, Cincinnati, and Lexington, and many cases appeared in the towns of the Great Miami Valley. Though a few citizens of Butler County died in this outbreak, the scattered population of the county remained almost uninfected.

This, however, was not true in 1834. In the southwestern part of the county, the highland in the northwestern part of Ross Township, and the eastern section of Morgan was stricken most severely.

I follow the account of William Bebb, later Governor of Ohio, as published in the Hamilton Intelligencer of July 31 and August 7, 1834.

The first case that occurred in the region infected was that of Reuben Woodruff, who had made a trip to Cincinnati, twenty-five miles away, where, according to the same issue of the Intelligencer, cholera deaths were occurring at the rate of about ten a week. He recovered because of skillful treatmen by his wife, who maintained the surface temperature of his body by packing around him bags of shelled corn, heated as hot as it could be endured.

The first death was that of his 7-year-old son who had been with him on the Cincinnati trip. The next death was that of a Mrs. Bell, a neighbor, and then that of her husband. During the illness at the Woodruff home, a Mr. Conley of Paddy's Run called there and after his return home he became ill and died.

This was the first case in Paddy's Run valley proper. Mrs. Maurice Jones sat up all night at the Conley's the night before Mr. Conley's death, was taken ill the next morning and died before night. Her husband, Maurice Jones, was attacked the next evening and died before morning.

Two of Mr. Conley's daughters, Ephraim Van Vickle and Ann Venable who were at his wake, Mr. Slingsby who made his coffin (and Mrs. Slingsby on authority of Chidlaw diary), and Abel Appleton and Martin Bissiers who were in attendance during his illness all died. Mr. Van Vickle became ill at Mr. Hidlay's, and at that home old Mr. Hidlay, old Mrs. Hidlay, young Mrs. Hidlay, and one not named, five in all, died. Squire Carmack's family, which lost four, were neighbors of the Hidlays and Venables. From Mr. Hidlay's the disease got into the family of Mr. Ent who lost, besides his daughter young Mrs. Hidlay, two other daughters, Mrs. Robeson and Miss Ent.

Dr. Kingsley, the Millville doctor, who was one of the early victims, I am told, had visited patients in the neighborhood where Mrs. and Mr. Bell died.

Whether Dr. Bottenberg had been exposed to the disease, Mr. Bebb did not know, but he presumed that because of his profession it was highly probable.

Old Mr. French was a neighbor of Mr. Bell and Mr. Ent. He and Foster Bails, who lived in the same house, died the same day. The son, Jeremiah French, and the daughter of Mr. French, Sr., were attacked the next day. The son died, the daughter recovered. During Jeremiah French's illness, his father-in-law, Henry Sefton, who lived in Hamilton County, five miles south of the infected region, visited him, was present at his death and burial, returned to his home in good health and the next day died after an illness of a few hours. His daughter, who had accompanied him to the funeral of Mr. French, also took the disease but survived. (The story was continued in the Intelligencer for August 7.)

Further deaths were those of Mrs. Abbott, a daughter of the Bells, Mrs. Hindman and Miss Hindman, Mrs. Robeson's child (age, sex unreported), Lydia Barns, a neighbor to the Doyles, Mr. Doyle (whose death was among the early ones), and Mr. Day, stepson of Mr. Doyle. From Crosby Township, Hamilton County—Deacon James C. Scott, of the Paddy's Run Church.

There seem to have been no more deaths in this locality after the issue of the Intelligencer for August 7, but by August 10 the disease appeared in Oxford, twelve miles north. The first death was in the family of Mr. E. Moore, that of his niece, Rebecca Scott. Mr. Moore's son died the next day after an attack of only eight hours. Mr. Moore and Julia Dean, the hired girl, died very shortly thereafter.

On August 12 the students at Miami University petitioned for the privilege of a dispersal (vacation) not to exceed four weeks to avoid the cholera then raging in Oxford. It was granted.

The Hamilton Intelligencer of September 4 reported as dead of the cholera in Oxford in addition to the four previously mentioned: Mrs. Duckett, William Adams, Mrs. William Adams and infant, Whitfield Washburn; Samuel Cory, the son of Dr. Cory; Mary Dowd, John T. Gause and Henry T. Barrows.

In addition to the Miami student body, half in the inhabitants of the village left town, the editor says. After the cholera scare was over and within their four-week limit, the Miami boys must have returned, for on September 23, there was an Erodelphian Literary Society anniversary in the afternoon and a Union Society meeting in the evening with Dr. Daniel Drake of Cincinnati as the orator. The next day, September 24, was the Commencement for the Class of 1834, when twenty-two were graduated, including at least three men nationally known later, W. S. Groesbeck, the Rev. J. G. Monfort, and the Rev. T. E. Thomas.

I have no means of tying up the Oxford infection with the one in Morgan and Ross Townships. There had been cholera in Hamilton in 1834, as well as in the summer of 1833. In these accounts I have omitted all the discussion concerning cause since the prevailing medical opinion had to do with the soil, the wind, the atmospheric changes and other similar non-essentials. Among seven different theories discussed by Daniel Drake the "animalcular" was introduced last and with seeming timidity. Most doctors also insisted that the disease was not contagious because you might be in the presence of a sufferer and still not take the disease. The first demonstration that cholera was actually water borne was twenty years later in the case of the Broad Street well in London. Even that preceded the formulation of the microbic theory of disease.

Cholera is caused by a spirillum which is transferred by contact, by flies, by uncooked food washed in infected water. Not every one takes cholera at a given time. It is more severe in those suffering from other intestinal troubles and in July, 1834, many might have had predisposing digestive upsets because of hot weather and lack of refrigeration for food.

There are no symptoms as long as the cholera germs remain in the intestine, since they produce no soluble toxins. But as the spirillum enters the epithelial cells of the intestines, these break down and then the toxins appear. The body flushes the intestinal tract, there is vomiting and the presence of "rice water" stools, the blood pressure drops, the urine ceases, and the fingers shrivel. There is marked acidosis, muscular cramping and the individual dies from excessive dehydration of the body. One of the treatments for cholera at present in the East is to inject serum or saline solution to prolong life so that medicine may have time to take effect.

One of the unconsidered protections against cholera in those days must have been the very common "chills, shakes or fever and ague." When Koch discovered the cholera organism fifty years later, he also found that a solution of $1/2500$ quinine sulphate would kill the cholera germ in ten to thirty minutes.

A modern cholera epidemic in Van, Turkey-in-Asia, was controlled in 1906 by quinine. More than 90 per cent of the patients, including those brought to the hospital moribund, recovered whereas with other treatment every patient during the first week succumbed.

When I lived as a boy in the Paddy's Run valley I had malaria. I was awakened at 4 a.m. on the "chill" day and given quinine wrapped in a wafer. This was repeated every hour thereafter until 9 o'clock, after which the dose was given every half hour until the onset of the fever. I do not know the size of the dose I was given, but many of the settlers, having acclimated their malarial parasites to mild quinine treatment, had to take enormous doses which would parallel the ten grains per hour which cured the Van patients in from four to eight hours. I assume that such malarial patients did not take the cholera.

I am presenting this paper for your criticism of my thesis that this particular epidemic was caused by transfer from house to house of a virulent phase of cholera from Cincinnati and by direct person to person infection rather than by infected wells or by flies. In the days before microbes were known the same dishes and especially the gourd or tin dipper in the water pail might have been used by the patient and the household at large hence the rapid succession of cases in single families.

The current use of home remedies, the habit of neighborly assistance in sickness and the ten-mile trip to call a physician and his ten-mile trip to his patient all speeded up the death of the most susceptible.

The very brief (three weeks) time of persistence of the epidemic does not give time enough to infect the separate wells where cases were found unless we assume that the infection of the whole area was made from cases in Hamilton the year before, that it wintered over and was washed into the wells by the heavy rains which are reported just at the start of the epidemic.

Cholera is not always malignant and the serious type usually becomes milder in a few weeks because by that time it is working on the less susceptible of the population.

The July 31 issue of the Intelligencer listed as having died in Morgan and Ross Townships of Asiatic cholera between July 10 and 31, 1834, the following:

John Woodruff (7), David Bell (60), Samuel Conley (the first on Paddy's Run proper) (45), Keiday Slingsby, Martin Bissiers (Busseur), Maurice Jones (65), Dr. Bottenberg (28), Old Mr. Hidlay (65), Ephraim Van Vickle (22), Mr. Sizelove, Mr. Venable (50), Mr. Rust, Abel Appleton (65), Foster

Bails (30), Old Mr. French (70), Jeremiah French (30), Carman Ross (60), Reuben Rude (70), Squire Carmack's son (15), Henry Sefton (65), Mr. Bissier's son (10), Mrs. Margaret Bell (55), Old Mrs. McCarty, Mrs. Maurice Jones (65), Mrs. Slingsby, Mrs. Baker, Mrs. Davis (30), Old Mrs. Hidlay (65), Young Mrs. Hidlay (35) born Ent, Mrs. Sizelove, Miss Conley (18), Miss Conley (15), Miss Ann Venable (18), Mrs. Williams (55), Old Mrs. Brenan, Miss Ent (18), Mrs. Robeson (40) born Ent, Miss Weaver, Mrs. Carmack (50), Miss Cone (20), Mrs. Faudree (25), and Miss Hindman.

The issue of the Intelligencer for August 7 added the following:

Mrs. Robeson's child, Mr. Day (23) stepson to Mr. Doyle, Deacon James C. Scott of Paddy's Run Church, Mrs. Abbott (35) born Bell, Mrs. Hindman (40), Lydia Barns, neighbor of the Doyles, and Miss Hindman (13).

Deaths totaled forty-nine.

McClelland chairs. 1 and 3 the Morgan Gwilym armchair. 2 and 6 the Evans rocker. 4, 5, 7 and 8 views of the Sefton rocker and straight chair. 9 the Francis rocker.

The Bebb clock. The John Halstead cherry and walnut desk-bookcase. The opened desk. Views of the toy Conestoga wagon made by Griffith

CHAPTER IX

EARLY CABINET MAKERS AND THEIR WORK

WE FIND no signed piece of furniture made in Paddy's Run and only a few whose complete history is known. Most of the men among these pioneers could make furniture as it was needed, but comparatively few had the skill or the time to make and finish elaborate pieces. Many of the wool spinning wheels were roughly put together; all that was asked of them was to produce thread. After wool spinning was a thing of the past, the steel spindle was removed and fashioned into a husking peg for corn and the stand and wheel were burned.

In our admiration for antiques we are likely to forget that our pleasure is based on the fact that the article still exists. When we find that the particular piece is still in daily use, a respect is added to our admiration which can never be elicited by an antique in a glass case in a museum.

Old furniture may be beautiful. Alas, it is often homely, but age in itself is a guarantee of a certain amount of honest handicraft and some care and interest in preservation. Continuous history of a piece of furniture may be considered a pedigree, and these pedigrees are often invalidated by fires, by public sales, or by a family dying out.

Among the interesting pieces made in the Paddy's Run valley is the Bebb clock, described by the Rev. Mr. Chidlaw as follows:

"A clock-case (now owned by descendants of Edward Bebb in Illinois) made by Stephen Hayden in 1804, shows the ingenuity and taste of this pioneer cabinet maker. It is made of cherry slabs, dressed as best he could, overcoming the want of sawmills with a whipsaw. Stephen Hayden, with such tools as he had, made a beautiful and neatly ornamented clock-case worthy of a place in the great Centennial Exhibit at Philadelphia. For many years it has been the cozy home of a brass clock which Mrs. Bebb brought from Wales in 1801. The face of the clock is 12 by 12 inches, but when the case was made the Cincinnati market could not furnish a piece of glass large enough to cover it. The glass is in two pieces, neatly joined by the hand of the skillful mechanic. This clock was a great curiosity to the Indians who frequently visited Mr. Bebb's cabin. He would make the clock strike around in their hearing but the children of the forest must have the cabin door open, that in case of danger they might seek safety in flight."

The descendants of John Halstead (1775-1855), still living on his half-section, have a number of well preserved examples of his skill. Among them are a desk-bookcase of cherry and walnut, a drop-leaf cherry table now in the home of Clarissa Scott Aberle in California, a walnut breakfast table, a large writing table, and two large movable cupboards which were built for the first floor room of the Halstead guest-house.

An excerpt concerning a local cabinet maker is taken from the autobiography of Mark Williams: "James Gilliland came from the South to avoid slavery and its effects, and his son was a life-long Abolitionist. Adam Gilliland was a good preacher, speaking without notes. He preached in the Bethel Church on Indian Creek as early as 1828 and in Venice 1839-1859. To supplement the pittance paid a minister he worked at cabinet making through the week for a number of years. As his family grew up to help, he cultivated a small farm near Venice. He lived to be ninety years old."

Isaac McClelland (1805-1887) was probably the best known of the local wood workers. He is said to have been a master hand at making spinning wheels, reels, bureaus, or sewing tables, but I know of no authentic specimens of his handiwork. There are, however, a number of chairs made by him so characteristic that they are still known as McClelland chairs by the families possessing them.

His son furnished this outline of his father's history: Born in Pennsylvania in 1805, his parents soon thereafter removed to the vicinity of Crawfordsville, Indiana. There he learned cabinet making, working with an older brother. He lived most of his active life near Richmond, Indiana, and Shandon, Ohio. He died at the age of 82 and is buried in Hamilton.

Isaac McClelland was locally famous, and was said by other mechanics to be so skilled a workman that he could do finer work with a drawing knife than other carpenters could with their planes.

His methods of making chairs is worthy of description in a day of machine made furniture. The rounds were turned out of well seasoned hickory and the posts were made of green maple. The dry round with a supply of the finest glue in a depression at each end was driven into green maple posts. As the posts seasoned they drew tightly about the round. Even in the modern, furnace heated homes McClelland's chairs are solid and the rounds are tight. The seats were made from strips of swamp ash and since his supply was kept in a neighboring creek, the material was always flexible for weaving.

A number of these original seats are in the chairs after a hundred years of service. Others have been replaced time after time by pith-cane, the usual material available in the market now for weaving seats. It does not compare in durability with the coarser ash, hickory, or white oak splits, which when put on with care outlast the average owner.

These chairs are, in general, of the ladder-back Colonial type, but no two are precisely the same in detail. I shall discuss a few of them, designating them for purposes of reference by the name of the original owner.

The John Evans chair, now in the possession of the family of a granddaughter, has a combination ladder and spindle back. The worn seat is not the original one and the rockers appear also not to be the original ones. The handgrasp at the end of the arm and the flare of the top are more pronounced in this chair than in any of the others. It is also the largest of the rocking chairs.

The Francis chair, a slat-back type, has had a series of rockers worn or broken and replaced. The top of the back has more of a backward curve than the other large chairs have. The handgrasps are worn off squarely in front, said to be due to the pushing of the chair about on rocker ends and arms while in the role of locomotive driven by the children of the house.

The Sefton chairs are probably among the latest made at Shandon (the present name of Paddy's Run). The set, rocker and six upright chairs, made for a wedding outfit in 1838, is still intact and with some of the original seats in place. The small chairs are shaped like the Francis rocker with bent back flaring somewhat at the ends. The rocker is like the Evans rocker but even more comfortable. No one who ever sat in that chair could forget the ease and the restfulness of the position. This chair is the only one of the larger chairs which has not had the original rockers worn away and replaced and it may be that this accounts for its extra comfort.

The Gwilym chair is unique. It is an upright armchair made for a stout man who did not care to trust himself to a rocker. It is as firm and strong now when climbed over by his great-great-great-grandchildren as it was the day it was delivered to him. The handgrasps are of a different type from those on the others shown and the uprights end in turned knobs. The original seat has been replaced.

The parts of these chairs worn by use have gained a polish and luster which is very attractive. The paint itself, where it is still present, has faded unobtrusively into the background, and the only one of the chairs which has been newly painted looks disturbed, as though it felt uncomfortable.

When one thinks of the furniture he has known in his own life it falls usually into two classes, the delicate and easily racked type and the huge, almost immovable pieces which occupy permanent positions, and are only disturbed for major cleaning operations. Isaac McClelland's chairs are of the first type in weight and appearance with the strength of the second, and they proclaim him a workman who needed not to be ashamed.

In 1839 Griffith M. Jones made for the oldest son of Deacon Hugh Williams a miniature Conestoga wagon; solid dished wooden wheels with iron tires, front axle with kingbolt, bolster and hounds, to turn freely. The back part of the wagon-bed extended upward to prevent loss of the load when going up steep hills. This wagon was used by Mark Williams when taking care of his younger brothers and sisters, as one now uses a baby carriage.

Mrs. Mary Bebb Vaughan had a cherry poster bed made about 1840 by a Mr. Cruson in New Haven. The sides were attached to the ends by screw threads cut in the wood, the interior threads cut in the bed ends and the exterior on the two ends of each of the sides. These threads had to be of opposite type on the two ends of the side so that both bed-ends could be engaged at the same time. By revolving the side in one direction it would tighten into both ends and by turning it in the opposite way it would loosen. How proud the pair of boys who succeeded in getting four fairly tight joints and then managed to lace in a firm but springy bottom with the family clothes line!

Mr. Halderman, the father of Cyrus Halderman in Venice, and Mr. Hawk, the great-grandfather of Mrs. Alma Joyce Scott, were early cabinet makers. Francis Kelshymer, of Venice, is said to have done fine inlaid work. He died in 1828 and his cabinet making tools were sold that fall by his executor.

There is a fine chest of drawers with inlaid work at the home of Edith and Crawford Morris. This may have been made in Cincinnati.

About 1870 David Griffith, who learned his trade in Cincinnati, built useful desk-bookcases for the Sefton, Evan Evans, and Francis families, and a walnut extension table for T. F. Jones, which is now the property of a member of the Wilkins family.

After these examples of skilled workmen and their work I am reminded of an ancestral clock, maker unknown, with all of the internal works of wood. My impression is that it never was a reliable time-piece and usually needed hospitalization. Finally it fell into the hands of a local amateur who never could get all the wheels back into the case in working order and the clock was ruined permanently. The famous student, assigned to produce a dog skeleton, who killed a second dog in order to find the correct locations for numerous problematical bones had a distinct advantage over this clock doctor.

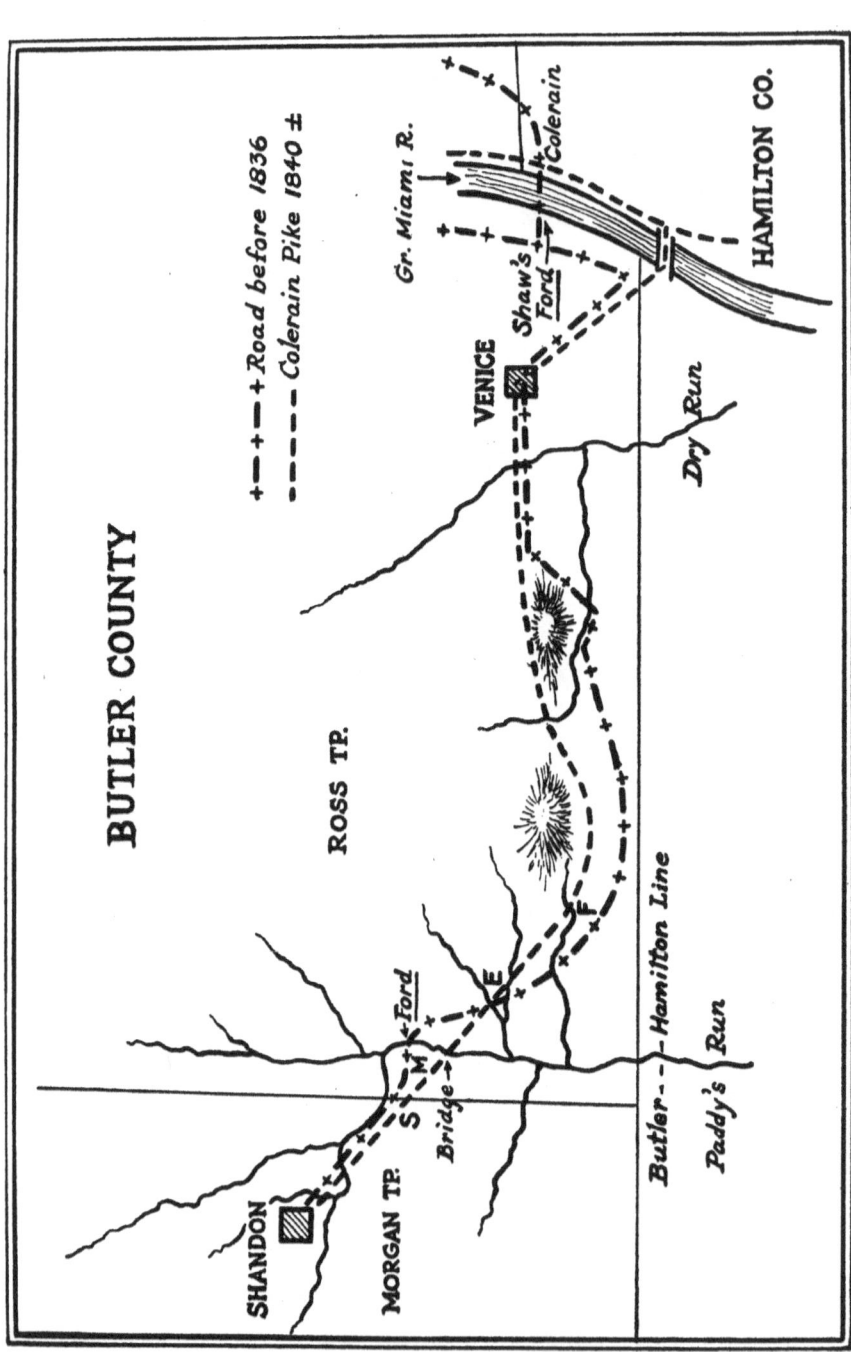

The earlier, more level road and the present Colerain Pike between Colerain and Shandon

CHAPTER X

THE ROADS, THE PIKE AND THE BUS

FOR the first few years after the settlers came to the Paddy's Run valley all traveling was on horseback along bridle paths with trees "blazed" here and there. According to Chidlaw, Morgan Gwilym brought the first two-horse wagon into the community in 1804 and after that time a passable road was one free from stumps and underbrush.

One of the early settlements in the valley was at Morgantown, site of the Hugh Smith grist mill in section 34 of Morgan Township, located on the post-glacial short-cut made by Dry Fork when it changed from a direct tributary of the ancestral Ohio to a branch of the Whitewater. This narrow valley and steep slope was a most favorable place for an inexpensive dam and a short race.

A mill was built sometime before 1808. I suppose that in the years before this the settlers used hand mills or mortar and pestle. The second building in this locality was John Iseminger's stillhouse, where corn whiskey sold for 12 to 18 cents a gallon. Wild or escaped peaches, plums, and black currants were also used in the manufacture of brandies.

George Iseminger in 1810 started a general store. Then a flax-seed oil mill by Smith and Robinson handled the by-product of the flax raised to be spun on the small wheel. Later a saw mill, a brewery, a blacksmith shop and an extensive cooper shop for barrels and buckets clustered around the grist mill nucleus. The oldest church building in the township was less than half a mile south on the other side of Dry Fork towards New Haven. No records have been left of the locations of the cabins of those who carried on these numerous manufacturing establishments, but all would add up to a pretentious village.

The surveyed road from Cincinnati to Brookville by-passed the rough country near Morgantown and the postoffice of

Tariff (1828) was established on that road three miles to the north. When Benjamin Lloyd platted a town near the post-office, by petition of the residents the name was changed to Okeana. In 1851-1853 a Methodist Church building was erected there to house the group which in 1817, in the Paddy's Run valley, were known as the Ephraim Carmack Society.

The probable base of the dam and traces of the mill-race on the east side of the Dry Fork, opposite the Easterbrooks' house, are the fossil remains of Morgantown.

The Old Road

In a deed for property in Paddy's Run, dated 1825, the road from Brookville to Cincinnati by Shaw's fording on the Great Miami is used as one of the boundaries. This crossing is shown on none of the maps accessible in Cincinnati, but is known to have been the usual route from the western part of Butler County and from much of southeastern Indiana to Cincinnati.

At the first public sale in Cincinnati of the land west of the Miami in 1801, Jeremiah Butterfield, Esquire Shaw and his sons Knowles and Albin, Asa Harvey and Noah Willey bought 2,000 acres of land extending south from the mouth of Indian Creek into Crosby Township of the present Hamilton County. A question was raised at Fort Hamilton as to whether they had a clear title. Albin Shaw was sent to Washington in 1804 and returned with the proper papers signed by Thomas Jefferson. After his return he parcelled out the land to the others, giving each a quitclaim deed. Since three out of the six men were named Shaw, it is natural to assume that one of the three may have owned the land where the wide, shallow crossing is located.

A mill above these shallows was built by Hyde in 1804. As it was sold to Samuel Dick in 1805 the ford has also gone under the name of Dick's Crossing.

The banks on each side had a gentle grade and the village of Colerain, east of the river, was on this Brookville road to Cincinnati. In later years when people wished to cross at all times, whether the ford was safe or not, a ferry was put in half a mile farther south where the stream was both narrower and deeper all the year round. In 1830 the first bridge was built at the point where the ferry had been running, the narrowness of the stream and the height of both banks making a favorable site for a bridge.

This bridge washed out in the 1832 flood and was replaced. Consequently, when the Colerain Pike was put in (1840) it crossed at this point and followed the river bank upstream through Colerain to ascend the hills to Dunlap.

Fortunately, James McBride, surveyor, made a map of Butler County in 1836, before the Colerain Pike was laid out in 1838-40. All the later township maps have been drawn to the scale he used, so it is a simple thing to trace both the road in 1836 and the pike as it now is from the Venice bridge to Shandon.

From the bridge to Venice and from that village to the foot of the hill half a mile west of it, the two roads are one. At that point the older road turned and followed the base of the hill to a cut made by a small stream south of the Brown farm. Leaving the Miami River bottoms by this cut, it curved around the foot of the ridge of hills east of the Paddy's Run valley, passing south of the John C. Jones log house and north and east of the David Francis house and the Richard Jones log house. Swinging eastward of the location of the future bridge it crossed the Paddy's Run at the ford back of the Morris house, went westward to cross the township road, up a sharp hill and down again straight into the village of Shandon.

The Colerain Pike took a much straighter course up the steep hill at the Orin Brown farm and then again up over the shoulder of the hills bounding the valley and on to cross a bridge over the Paddy's Run and coincide with the old road from where it crossed the township line on into the village.

The James Shields house, built in 1819, was set with reference to the hill rather than to either road. As it used a short lane as entrance, the only change that was made as long as the house stood, was to move the lane from the township road to the pike at the point of its starting to ascend the hill.

From the point of view of ups and downs the old road had a distinct advantage over the straighter Colerain Pike. The pike was constructed so early, however, that no house but that of David Francis was left badly isolated. That was replaced by the present Francis house in 1857-8.

From Paddy's Run the old road extended northwest for a mile or more to the DeArmond hill and turned sharply west to pass by the Hickory Chapel of the Rev. Rees Lloyd. Then it turned northwest until it reached Dry Fork and followed the right bank northward to unite with the road from New Haven after it crossed the creek. Here a long straight section is still known as Race Lane. Above this point the road reached the postoffice of Tariff. When the Cincinnati-Brookville pike was put through, it followed a shorter path from DeArmond's over the hills directly through the site of Tariff to the present Okeana.

The Colerain Pike from Cincinnati to Brookville, Indiana, (a branch ran from Venice to Oxford) was under construction for a number of years in the latter part of the 1830's. It was built by a stock company. Since counties and townships did not have enough money to finance all their necessities at once, toll-roads, such as this one, sprang up in the parts of the state which were settled.

These roads were, as a rule, well made and carefully cared for, answering their purpose at the time adequately. After 1900 these toll-roads were gradually bought up by the State, and the same people who objected to paying the charges at the tollgates were shortly vociferously complaining of the depreciation of the roads when they were no longer kept in good condition by the stock companies.

In 1847 a daily bus line was started on the Colerain Pike from Paddy's Run through Venice, Dunlap, Bevis, Groesbeck, and Mt. Airy to Cincinnati, a distance of twenty miles. (At an earlier date there was a bus from Cincinnati to Brookville one day and from Brookville to Cincinnati the next day.) This line continued for fifty years under a number of managements. One team of horses would work to Bevis in the early morning, leaving Paddy's Run at about 6 o'clock and then return about 6 in the evening, while the horses which took on at Bevis for Cincinnati brought the bus back to that point from the city in the afternoon. Numerous long and steep hills along the route made the journey a dangerous one when there was ice on the road and when the first and last parts of the day's travel were necessarily in the dark.

For many years Jesse Bevis and his successors as bus drivers were the connection between Paddy's Run and waystations to Cincinnati. When the early railways were built in the 1850's, the nearest stations (Hamilton and Harrison) were each ten miles away. It was the next century before a railroad was built through Shandon (Paddy's Run) itself.

Much of the village activity centered about the bus. It carried the mail, brought the newspapers, and did a general express business for small articles. When there was no resident pastor the supplying minister came on the Saturday afternoon bus from Cincinnati and in the winter time left before daylight Monday morning. Many Lane Seminary students preached their first sermons in the Paddy's Run Congregational Church, and on the other hand, men as famous as Lyman Beecher were also available.

At rare intervals a larger, heavier bus needing four horses had to be used and the driver with the double sets of lines to handle was apt to alarm nervous passengers. One time this large bus was late and making up time into the village and a small boy ran up the street yelling: "Here comes George Patton with the four-horse bus lickety-split and old Mr. Cisle inside with his eyes as big as dinner plates!"

The Legislature in 1844 set a schedule of prices to be charged by the stock companies controlling toll-roads. They were for each ten miles traveled on the road:

Four-wheeled wagons with two horses, 15 cents, with 5 cents for each additional horse; sled or sleigh with two horses, 10 cents, with 5 cents for each additional horse; horse and rider, 5 cents; four-wheeled carriage, one horse, 15 cents, for two horses, 25 cents; two-wheeled gig with one horse, 10 cents, 15 cents for two horses; cart same as gig; horse or mule six months or over, 3 cents each; each head of neat cattle (driven), 1 cent; each head of sheep or hogs (driven), ½ cent.

Regular patrons were permitted to pay by the year and at a lower rate.

CHAPTER XI

THE MILITIA

BEFORE Wayne's treaty with the Indians in 1795, all able-bodied men in Ohio were potential soldiers (militia). The War of 1812 produced again marauding bands of Indians in the pay of the British and again most of the physically able were called to fight.

In 1792, because of the foresight of President Washington and others, a plan for training a citizen soldiery was prepared. Following this plan the Legislature of Ohio, and I suppose those of other states, constituted the whole male population between 18 and 45 years (with certain exceptions) into a militia organization, one regiment for each county. This regiment was supposed to drill publicly one day each year, Battalion Day.

In 1828 the Ohio militia consisted of 4 major generals, 48 brigadier generals, 146 colonels, 182 lieutenant colonels, 183 majors, 1,406 captains, and 94,046 privates.

There were 129 regiments of regular infantry, 8 of light infantry, 28 of riflemen, 17 of cavalry, and 28 of artillery. In many counties special regiments of volunteers, required to furnish uniforms and to drill more often, were arranged for.

In 1827 and after such a regiment had its drill ground at Millville. Abner Francis of Ross was a captain, William Bebb of Morgan the adjutant and Griffin Halstead of Ross, colonel. These officers dressed their part. Years after, at a public sale a sword, belt and sash—the gold on the latter much tarnished—was sold for a small sum and was later used by small boys in playing war.

Brigade orders, published July 13, 1829, in the Hamilton Intelligencer, read: "The commissioned and staff officers of the Third Brigade, 1st div., Ohio Militia will assemble in Rossville the 14th & 15th of August next, armed and equipped according to law for the purpose of a Brigade Officer Muster. —R. B. Millikin, Brigadier General."

In 1832 an editorial in the Intelligencer says: "No system for the general training of all our citizens can be carried into effect." There was also a notice published in the early summer of 1832 that the Miami Guards and Miami Blues (special regiments) were to parade on the Fourth of July and that the surviving Revolutionary soldiers were to march in a procession at that celebration.

By that time the Battalion Day in the fall had degenerated into a frolic and a family good time, marked by horse trading and dancing rather than military training.

The only Paddy's Run citizen serving in the War of 1812 was Major Charles Ent, born New Jersey in 1767. He moved his family to Ohio about 1818. He died June 20, 1847. After the new cemetery in Paddy's Run was opened his body and that of his wife were moved to this burying ground.

Thomas Owens, buried in the southeast corner of the old graveyard, was a soldier in the Mexican War. He had been wounded and was left with a crippled hand which prevented him from doing farm work. He was employed in Henry Robinson's store, but discouraged by his future prospects, he took poison and killed himself, age 37 years, 2 months, on June 24, 1852.

James T. Patton, who died July 30, 1922, aged 92, was in the Fourth Ohio Infantry in the Mexican War in 1846 and in the Hundred Days service in 1864.

Almost all of the Morgan Township men who enlisted in the Third Ohio in 1861 at the call of President Lincoln for 75,000 men, re-enlisted at the end of the three months into Company H, Fifth Ohio Volunteer Cavalry, for three years. Many continued to the end of the war.

In the Infantry were: The Rev. B. W. Chidlaw, Chaplain 39th O. V. I. under Col. John Groesbeck and later Col. A. W. Gilbert. Resigned April 9, 1862, to enter U. S. Christian Commission, 1862-1865.

Fred D. McKasson, Co. C, 35th reg, O. V. I. under Colonel Vanderveer.

THE MILITIA 79

Martin McKasson, 3rd Ohio, re-enlisted in an Illinois cavalry regiment.

Benton Halstead (see Chapter XIII and special biography in Chapter XIV).

W. L. Brown, Co. C, 69th O. V. I., died May 8, 1862; buried in old graveyard.

W. L. Milholland, Co. C, 69th O. V. I.

Thomas Bebb, Co. B, 87th O. V. I., buried in old graveyard.

J. T. DeArmond, Co. F, 93rd O. V. I.

167th O. V. I. (100 Days Men, 1864):

Company A: Peter Brooks.

Company B: Capt. Edward T. Jones, 1st Lieut. Sam W. Woodruff, 2nd Lieut. W. Crosby Vaughan (buried in new cemetery), Sgt. David Mering (see Co. H, Fifth O. V. C.), Sgt. James Scott (buried in new cemetery), Sgt. Isaac Erven, Sgt. James DeArmond, Cpl. Maurice Jones (buried in old graveyard), and Cpl. James E. Bebb.

Privates were: Abel Appleton, Jr., Thomas Bebb (see Co. B, 87th O. V. I.), William Breese, Morgan Davies, Thomas Davies, A. W. DeArmond, William A. Dusenberry (see Co. H, Fifth O. V. C.), Daniel Griffith (drowned 1866, buried in old graveyard), Henry Hall (buried in new cemetery), Evan Howell (buried in new cemetery), Andrew J. Jones (buried in new cemetery), John L. Jones, Michael Jones (buried in new cemetery), William Lewis, W. T. Lloyd, (Allen) Gilson Morris (buried in new cemetery), James T. Patton (see Mexican War; new cemetery), William Rees, John T. Roberts, Maurice Roberts, and Andrew J. Youmans (buried in new cemetery).

Company K: James A. Clark (buried in new cemetery).

Serving in the Fifth Ohio Volunteer Cavalry were: Col. W. H. H. Taylor, Captain Murray, Richard Griffith (promoted to 1st Lieutenant Co. G); David Mering, Quartermaster Sergeant (see 167th Ohio Co. B); James T. Bell, Quartermaster Sergeant; Abner F. Davis, Battalion Sergeant Major; John J. Evans, Sergeant; John O. Evans, Sergeant; Richard J. Nicholas, Sergeant (from Gomer, Ohio); Everett Sefton, Sergeant (buried in new cemetery); Thomas A. Thomas, Sergeant (died, Corinth, Miss., 1862); Rees H. Evans, Corporal (captured December 1862, exchanged); William C. Evans, Corporal; Sam Howell, Corporal; John H. Jones, Corporal; John O. Morgan, Corporal; John Milholland, Corporal; Evan W. Davies, Farrier (buried in new cemetery); John D. Davies, Farrier.

Privates: John Abraham, John Bevin (buried in new cemetery), William Black, Richard Breese, David W. Davies, William A. Dusenberry (also 167th Ohio Co. B), John B. Evans (buried in new cemetery), William G. Evans, Evan Griffith, John Griffith (drowned 1866, buried in old graveyard), Richard L. Hughes, Israel Jones, John J. Jones (buried in new cemetery), John W. Jones, James W. Jones, Morris S. Jones, and William T. Lewis (promoted to 1st Lieutenant and Adjutant), 110th regiment (colored), Richard Manuel (buried in new cemetery), William Manuel (buried in new cemetery), Francis McBride (buried in old graveyard), John H. Morris (buried in new cemetery?), Thomas M. Morris, John Reese, Richard Rowland (buried in new cemetery), Evan B. Thomas, William W. Tudor, and Evan R. Watkins.

It is unfortunate that Will T. Lewis and David W. Davies are the only men of Company H of the Fifth Ohio Cavalry (except for those who enlisted in the Hundred Days service after their three years were up) whose names are inscribed on the walls of the Butler County Soldiers' Monument in Hamilton (1944).

War Stories

The following stories came from different sources as the records of the soldiers were sent to the author. Seventy years ago there would have been hundreds like them told at every G. A. R. reunion.

William Manuel was doing picket duty in northern Mississippi in the region of Corinth, when a detachment of Confederates attacked. His horse either fell or was shot—he did not stop to see, but ran into a cornfield and distanced his pursuers who were between him and the Northern camp. He ventured at dusk to go to a house and found that it was occupied by two sisters, Northern sympathizers, whose brother had just died. When the Confederate detachment came by later the women knew nothing of the whereabouts of any Northern soldier. After they had gone Manuel went into the house and was concealed there for three nights, spending the days in a cornfield. When on the fourth day he risked going back to the Union camp where he had been given up as dead or captured, a wild whoop of joy was set up by his partners in Company H.

Richard Manuel was in Sherman's march to the sea. At Resaca or some one of the engagements before Atlanta, the company was withdrawing hastily before a Confederate charge when Manuel's horse fell, probably shot. As he got up, somewhat dazed, he instinctively started to collect his saddle and bridle, but his mates yelled at him to grab a stirrup instead, which he did and so avoided capture.

Bachgen Jones (Bachgen means boy in Welsh) moved with his family to Allen County in the forties and went into the army from there. While camped in the West Virginia mountains, his outfit built fires by day on large stones so that sentinels on guard at night could have warm places on which to stand.

In the march on Atlanta, near Big Shanty, Jones was shot by a rebel up in a tree. His comrade shot the rebel and then seeing how seriously Jones was wounded, shook hands with him and ran for help. Before the surgeon reached him, Jones had bled to death.

Morgan's Raid, 1862

The main body of Confederates in Morgan's Raid passed south of Paddy's Run through New Haven, burned the Great Miami bridge at New Baltimore and continued until they reached the edge of Cincinnati, which they by-passed, realizing that it would be easy to enter but difficult to get out. The word of their coming preceded them by a number of hours.

Deacon Hugh Williams had time to send his farm horses to his woods north of the village, leaving them in the care of his 12-year-old son, Roger. About daylight the next morning Union soldiers under General Hobson came down the Okeana road, and inspecting every woods-pasture, found the horses and took three of them for remounts in spite of the tears of the boy. They gave him in return, however, a signed slip of paper, which was redeemed by the U. S. Government in 1869 at $125 for each horse taken.

At the Francis farm the horses were fastened in a space cut out in the center of a cornfield far away from the woods and were not discovered.

CHAPTER XII

NAMES OF THE PADDY'S RUN POSTOFFICE

IN THE early years of the community of Paddy's Run mail was received at Cincinnati, Harrison, or Hamilton and was called for and distributed by any of the villagers having business in those places. Mail was expensive and when one of the Jones' was charged more than a dollar for a letter from a relative in Wales and found it to be original poetry in Welsh, he naturally was aggrieved and the story got around.

As the community grew it needed more direct connection with the outside world and June 10, 1831, the Paddy's Run postoffice was established, with William Vaughan the first postmaster, an office which he held for nearly twenty years. After his death his wife carried on for a time. John L. Evans was postmaster under President Fillmore and later under Lincoln and Grant. A letter of Roger Williams' from Germany in 1872 gives credit to Alex Guthrie for obtaining the first canceling stamper with the name Paddy's Run. Previously the postmaster evidently canceled by hand.

As long as the villagers remained where the name was familiar it attracted no comment, but soon young people began going away for more advanced study than the local school afforded.

The first young man to go to college gave his name and home in a meeting and was greeted with roars of laughter and deafening stamps on the chapel floor. With few exceptions these men from Paddy's Run were named at once for the duration of their college life, Paddy Jones or whatever the Welsh surname happened to be. Miss Peabody, head of the Western Seminary, would not use the name at all, but printed one of the other names by which the village was known, New London, in all her catalogues.

I quote from the autobiography of Mark Williams, one of the early college graduates from the community in a course other than medicine: "In the spring vacation of 1857 I tried to have the name of our postoffice changed from Paddy's Run to some better sounding name. (He had just taught three months in the more advanced room of the local district school.) I wrote a dialogue for two of my former pupils in order to introduce the subject and then Abner Jones (also Miami '58) and I were to urge the people to make the change. The community was notified that we would make addresses on Friday night. Only Rev. Mr. Pryse was let into the secret. Not having had time to commit my address, I read it. It was on the 'Dignity of Labor.' Then Jones spoke. The dialogue followed, the intention of which was to show that the name Paddy's Run was ridiculous and mortifying to students who went abroad to school, making them a reproach by causing them to be called 'Paddies.' Then Mr. Pryse made a speech in our favor and so did Dr. G. M. Shaw.

"But the stay-at-homes, like John L. Evans, didn't like to be caught by guile, and, aggrieved that others should seem to control them, objected and induced the hangers on about the groceries to oppose the proposed change.

"Also many of our older citizens were averse, thinking that pride was at the bottom of our desire. So the movement was halted, but the attention of all was called to the subject and persons had committed themselves to one side or the other.

"During vacation I composed my first poem, called out by this experience. It was called 'Paddy's Run' and was supposed to be written by an opponent speaking of the shallow-pated college boys who wanted to change a time-honored name. Though the villagers disclaimed being descendants of Patrick, the name was dear to them. This poem was dedicated to Col. Griffin Halstead, the pillar of conservatism.

> It's the last of July and the midst of vacation,
>   And every one's seeking his fun;
> No tumult now vexes our glorious nation,
>   Nor the people of Paddy's Run.
> Last spring, we assembled to listen to speeches,
>   When an unlooked-for attempt was begun
> By upstarts from college, too big for their breeches,
>   To change our old name—Paddy's Run.
> They failed in their efforts and couldn't quite come it,
>   Though the doctor and preacher spoke long,

> If words had prevailed, they surely had won it,
>   But our hatred of change was too strong.
> It waters our cows, and it runs past our houses,
>   And we think it a good enough name.
> It's just as familiar as a pair of old trousers,
>   And we want it kept always the same.
> The unfortunate Paddy, who was drowned in its waters,
>   Has his memory embalmed in our name,
> But we surely won't say we're his sons and his daughters,
>   For from Wales all our ancestors came.
> Though people abroad may think we are Paddies,
>   They come far enough from the truth;
> They're deceived by the name, both our mammies and daddies
>   Came over from Wales in their youth.
> We're proud of our valley, and proud of our people,
>   And we hope they'll keep always the same,
> Of our library, schoolhouse, and handsome church steeple,
>   And last of all, proud of our name.
> Those boys got the big-head who went off to college,
>   And thought theirs a job easy done,
> But failed to convince us with all their great knowledge,
>   And we'll keep our old name, Paddy's Run.
>
> —Mark Williams (1857)

"In 1863 I had an urgent call to teach the select school in the village as their teacher had disappointed them. The school was a success in numbers and paid the trustees. After my school closed in 1864 I made a second attempt, without planning with others, to change the name of the postoffice. I had some advocates, but John L. Evans mustered his adherents and the way was blocked, but it helped toward future success."

The third and first successful trial at change of name of the postoffice came in 1886. A petition, signed by some influential citizens, to the Postmaster General requested that the name of Paddy's Run postoffice be changed to Glendower. (The name which had been proposed previously was Cambria.) Letters favoring this change were written by many outsiders, including the superintendent of rural mail service at Cincinnati, Congressman Butterworth of Hamilton County; L. D. Brown, state school commissioner; D. W. McClung of Cincinnati, former teacher in the Paddy's Run school; ex-Governor George Hoadly; and the Rev. B. W. Chidlaw, Miami 1833, a former pastor in Paddy's Run.

The local postmistress, Miss Carrie Hieatt, also favored the change of name.

Official information from Washington of the change of name of the postoffice from Paddy's Run to Glendower was the first news most of the residents of the village received and the Battle of Glendower was on.

Close friends became enemies, political ties were shattered and families divided on the question. Petitions were circulated, with one accommodating young fellow signing both for and against, making a congressional pair of himself. To hold her job, the postmistress withdrew her earlier letter, saying that a large majority of her patrons preferred the old name. Small boys having no votes or petitionary rights fought each other, which probably did a great deal of good in letting off steam.

Butler County is a natural stronghold of the Democratic party in Ohio and at the time James E. Campbell was the district's Representative in Washington. In some way a petition for returning to the Paddy's Run name was either miscounted or discounted by his clerk, a mistake which was greatly to his disadvantage.

In general, those of the community with more connection with the outside world were willing to lose the stigma of coming from Paddy's Run while the greater number, those who stayed more closely at home where the name was familiar, gloried in their unique postoffice name.

The adherents of the old name met as a town meeting in the old church, now the community house, and after much vocal fireworks, unanimously adopted these resolutions: "Whereas, The name of our postoffice has been changed from Paddy's Run to Glendower, largely through the offensive interference of men high in political standing: and whereas, this action is in direct opposition to the wishes of a large majority of the citizens, who alone are concerned, Now, therefore, be it resolved, That we denounce as false and unmanly the assertion of Hon. Benjamin Butterworth, that any man that has any appreciation of the decency and proprieties of life desires the name changed, and Resolved, that ex-Governor Hoadly, in asserting that the name of Paddy's Run is absurd

NAMES OF THE PADDY'S RUN POSTOFFICE   87

and distasteful to the people, makes a statement that cannot be substantiated; and Be it further Resolved, that notwithstanding the claims of the Hon. James E. Campbell (that he had been in no way responsible, for the change) whether innocent or guilty, he is largely responsible, on account of his inconsistent action, for the dark clouds of suspicion now resting upon him."

At the same time they addressed the following letter to Adlai E. Stevenson, First Assistant Postmaster General: "Dear Sir: Inasmuch as the name of our postoffice has been changed to Glendower against the will of a vast majority of its patrons, we, the undersigned, who have been receiving mail at this address for more than fifty years, believe that the underlying principles of our Republic have been violated and we believe that it is our privilege and duty to seek redress. We, therefore, respectfully request you to revoke your late action, brought about by the malicious statements of men of political prominence, who neither care what our office is called, nor know the feelings of our people in this regard, by restoring the name of Paddy's Run."

After a continuous and wordy siege in the newspapers and by letter for fifteen months, the Postoffice Department surrendered unconditionally and in January, 1888, Paddy's Run displaced the name of Glendower for the oldest Welsh settlement in Ohio. There was a day of cannonading, band-playing, and rejoicing of the majority in the old valley.

Murat Halstead, as the self-appointed historian of this bitter conflict, said: "There never was as much feeling exercised both for and against such a small affair as this since the establishment of the Postoffice Department and it is hoped that never will such be manifested again." (Commercial Gazette, January 28, 1888.)

Within five years, after the death of some of the old guard and the removal of others to distances at which they could note the obloquy of hailing from Paddy's Run, a quiet note from the Postoffice Department stated that, if from a list of more euphonious names, not including the two conflicting ones, a name could be selected that would satisfy both factions, the department stood ready to settle the matter. The name Shandon, pleasing to both sides as being Irish enough to suit Paddy's Run enthusiasts and attractive enough so that persons hailing from there did not automatically have the finger of scorn pointed at them, was selected.

At the present time this much named community on the Paddy's Run, locally known as New London from the time of the Select School of the Rev. Thomas Thomas in 1821, Bagdad to the boys of the Sycamore Grove School of William Bebb, 1828-1832, Paddy's Run (postoffice) 1831-1886, Glendower, 1886-1888, Paddy's Run 1888-1893, and Shandon from 1893, is carrying on as it has for nearly one hundred and fifty years as a part of our democracy.

List of the postmasters of Paddy's Run, Glendower, and Shandon:

William Vaughan, June 10, 1831; H. H. Robinson, January 20, 1848; John L. Evans, March 15, 1852; H. H. Robinson, August 8, 1853; John L. Evans, July 25, 1861; A. H. Guthrie, December 4, 1871; W. C. Vaughan, October 16, 1879; Ann T. Price, November 3, 1880; Carrie Hieatt, who served for Paddy's Run, Glendower and Paddy's Run; Samuel Cisle; Carrie Hieatt for Shandon; Frank Colborn, and John Guthrie, 1908 to 1940, when he was retired for age.

CHAPTER XIII

SONS AND DAUGHTERS OF THE COMMUNITY

THE LIST of professional and business men from the community, including those from nearby villages who attended the Paddy's Run schools, includes:

MINISTERS FROM THE COMMUNITY

Thomas Ebenezer Thomas, born Chelmsford, England, December 23, 1812. Miami, 1834. Presbyterian pastor; president, Hanover College; professor, New Albany Theological Seminary, displaced because of anti-slavery attitude; professor at Lane Theological Seminary until his death February 3, 1875.

B. W. Chidlaw, born Bala, Wales, July 14, 1811. Miami, 1833. Pastor, Paddy's Run, 1836-1843; missionary American Sunday School Union; Chaplain, 39th Regiment, O. V. I., 1861-1862; U. S. Christian Commission, 1863-1865. Trustee of Miami University, 1863 until death, July 14, 1892, while on a visit to his birthplace in Wales.

Abner F. Jones, born Paddy's Run, June 25, 1833. Miami, 1858; Lane Seminary, 1861. Congregational pastor, Columbia, Ohio. Enlisted with his parishioners in the Hundred Days service, 1864; died in this service August 12, 1864.

Mark Williams, born Paddy's Run, October 28, 1834. Miami, 1858; Lane Seminary, 1861. Congregational pastor; missionary to North China, 1866 to his retirement. One of the last to go by sailing ship around the Cape of Good Hope. Died August 9, 1920, on steamer returning to China.

William T. Lewis. Soldier in Civil War, 1861-1865, Fifth Ohio Volunteer Cavalry, later promoted to 1st Lieutenant and Adjutant of U. S. 110th Regiment (colored); law student, then ordained to the ministry of the Methodist Church by its West Virginia Conference in 1872. Pastorates in West Virginia, Ohio, Missouri, Arkansas, Delaware, Maryland, and Pennsylvania. No information after 1910.

Thomas J. McClelland, born Paddy's Run. Miami, 1868. Presbyterian pastor, Ohio and Indiana. Died Newark, Ohio, 1922.

Spencer E. Evans, born Paddy's Run, June 12, 1868. Marietta, 1891; Yale Divinity School, 1895. Congregational pastor, Granby and Terryville, Connecticut, for more than forty years. Died Granby, Connecticut, August 16, 1939.

J. Charles Evans, born Paddy's Run, February 26, 1867. Miami, 1895; Chicago Divinity School, 1898. Congregational pastor, Illinois, twelve years; North Dakota, seven years; a number of pastorates in Washington state, where (1944) he is still actively at work. Received D.D. degree, 1924, Miami University.

E. Walter Scott, born, Lebanon, Ohio, December 12, 1876. Marietta, 1900; Yale Divinity School, 1904. Chaplain in U. S. Navy, 1904 until retirement in 1940 with rank of Captain. D.D., 1923, Marietta.

MISSIONARIES

Mark Williams (see Ministers).

Clarinda Wilkins Langridge, born June 17, 1836. A member of the second class to graduate from the Western Female Seminary at Oxford. Taught Freedmen schools many years and with her husband, brother and sister founded the Langridge School in Montgomery, Alabama. Married John Langridge, July 14, 1879. Died May 31, 1896.

Elizabeth Wilkins Tweedy, born March 4, 1841. Lebanon Normal School, Lebanon, Ohio. Helped her sister in the government schools to which they went as missionaries and in the Langridge School. Married James Madison Tweedy, April 2, 1874. Died Montgomery, Alabama, February 14, 1891.

Ann Wilkins, born August 8, 1846. Lebanon Normal School, Lebanon, Ohio. Taught in private school and among the Negroes five years. Died February 14, 1931.

John Wilkins, born August 2, 1851. Lebanon Normal School. Taught in government schools in Montgomery, Alabama, and assisted in organizing the Langridge School. Died October 21, 1942.

SONS AND DAUGHTERS OF THE COMMUNITY

Anna B. Jones, born May 2, 1862. Granville Female College, 1883. Taught in Lima, Ohio, for three years and for forty years in mission schools in or near Constantinople, Turkey. Retired 1930.

Henrietta B. Williams, born September 25, 1867, Kalgan, China. Western Female Seminary, 1886; Oberlin, 1889. Taught in Santee Agency Indian School, Nebraska, 1889-1892. Sent to China by the Woman's Board of Missions, 1893, stationed in Kalgan, where she died of typhus fever, May 30, 1898.

Emily Williams Harding, born May 26, 1873, in Peking, China. Oberlin, 1898. Married Dr. George Harding June 29, 1900. They were sent as medical missionaries to India. In Ahmednager, Dr. Harding died of blood poisoning from an infection, January 14, 1903. Their son George was born March 15, 1903. Mrs. Harding supervised school and orphanage in Sholapur, 1904-1907. Returned to the U. S. via China, 1907-1908. Taught in Santee Agency, Nebraska, 1909-1918. On Oberlin library staff from 1920 to retirement. Since then librarian, Thorsby Institute, Thorsby, Alabama.

Mary Williams Hemingway, born August 3, 1875, in Kalgan, China. Oberlin, 1899. Married Dr. Willoughby A. Hemingway, October 3, 1903. They were sent as medical missionaries to TaiKu, Shansi, China, where Dr. Hemingway established the Judson Smith Memorial Hospital, having charge of the institution until his death, November 9, 1932. Mrs. Hemingway continued in China with two of her daughters until they insisted that she return on the last open trip of the President Coolidge in May, 1941. Her daughters came from China on the exchange ship Gripsholm in 1942. Mrs. Hemingway was retired August 1, 1943. Address, 701 Shepherd Street, Washington, D. C.

Lawyers from the Community

William Bebb, born on Dry Fork, Morgan Township, December 8, 1802. Taught state and private school, 1826-1832. Admitted to the bar, 1831; practiced in Hamilton to 1850. Public speaker, Governor of Ohio, 1847-1848. Land owner in Illinois; colonizer, Tennessee, 1858-1861; Patent Office examiner, Washington, to 1869. Died Illinois, October 23, 1873.

James Nicholas, born Paddy's Run, September 6, 1810. (Included among the lawyers because during his more than fifty years service as justice of the peace in Allen County, his endeavors were always to have the parties compromise their difficulties, and though he wrote more wills than any other justice in the county, there was never a will written by Squire Nicholas broken by the courts.) Died, 1894.

Alfred Thomas, born Knottingly, England, February 15, 1815. Miami, 1837. In the law section of the U. S. Treasury Department until retirement. Died December 11, 1903.

Benton Halstead (see chapter XIV). Practiced law in Cincinnati and Washington, D. C.

Edward N. Evans, born Paddy's Run, 1845. Miami, 1870. Practiced law, Emporia, Kansas, from 1877 until his death, January 28, 1930.

John Elbert Sater, born New Haven, Hamilton County, January 16, 1854. Marietta, 1875. Superintendent of schools, 1875-1881; chief clerk, office State Commissioner of Schools, 1881-1884. Admitted to bar, 1884; member and president Columbus Board of Education; U. S. District judge, Southern Ohio, 1907-1924, resigned to practice law. LL.D., Miami, 1911. Died July 18, 1937.

Edward H. Jones, born Gomer, Ohio, 1865. Student at Miami, 1890; Cincinnati Law School, 1891. Practice, Hamilton and Cincinnati; probate judge, Butler County, 1899-1905; judge Court of Appeals, six years; judge of Circuit Court. Died, Cincinnati, 1926.

Homer Morris, born Paddy's Run, August 8, 1868. Marietta, 1890; Harvard Law School, 1893. Practice, Cincinnati, Ohio, and Minneapolis, Minnesota.

Clarence M. Humes, born September 10, 1868, Urbana, Ohio. Marietta, 1888. Teacher 1888-1903; practiced law, Chattanooga, Tennessee. Died February 16, 1939.

Lowry F. Sater, born New Baltimore, Hamilton County, Ohio, 1869. Ohio State, 1895. Law practice, Columbus, Ohio. LL.D., Miami, 1929. Died 1935.

U. F. (1866-1928) and Ben Bickley (1877-1942), law partners, Hamilton, Ohio, 1894-1928.

SONS AND DAUGHTERS OF THE COMMUNITY 93

A. W. Duvall, born Paddy's Run. Miami, 1909; LL.B. Detroit College of Law, 1914. Taught in Ohio, 1904-1906, Wisconsin 1909, Wyoming 1911. Practiced law, Salt Lake City, Utah, two years in office of prosecuting attorney in Salt Lake City. Practicing in Hamilton and Oxford at present.

Carl Teetor, born May 26, 1891. Student at Miami University, 1908-1910; LL.B., Michigan, 1912. Practicing Hamilton and Okeana; justice of the peace.

William Schradin. Student at University of Michigan; University of Cincinnati, LL.B., 1917. In business in Cincinnati, 1920-1941. Assistant personnel manager, Wright Aero Corporation, Lockland plant, 1941-1944. Investment business in Cincinnati, 1944————.

Doctors from the Community

John Halstead, Jr., born 1804. Attended Miami University; M.D., Ohio Medical College, 1828 or 1829. Died Indiana, 1846.

John Fletcher Shaw, born January 19, 1813. M.D., Ohio Medical College, 1836. Died 1836.

Griffin M. Shaw, born February 24, 1817. Studied with Dr. Cyrus Falconer and Dr. Daniel Drake. M.D., Ohio Medical College, 1841. Practiced Noblesville, Indiana, until 1854. Returned to Paddy's Run 1854, bought the house in the fork between the pikes in the village of Paddy's Run from Hugh Williams, built a brick office and later purchased all the land up to the lane by the church. He was a draft board officer for Morgan Township in the Civil War until his sudden death from appendicitis in 1863.

John and William B. Davis, brothers and partners. Dr. William B. was a professor in the Miami Medical College up to the late 1880'.s

John Milholland (1843——?—). M.D., Miami Medical College. Practised, Winterset, Iowa, near Des Moines.

Thomas S. Roberts (1844-1919). Son of Dr. Joseph Roberts and Sarah Halstead Roberts. Attended Miami University. M.D., Ohio Medical College. Practised, Illinois and South Dakota. Died Long Beach, California, 1919.

William Milholland (1848——?—). M.D., Miami Medical College. Practised Pemberton and Sidney, Shelby County, Ohio.

John W. Bell (1851-1931). M.D., Miami Medical College, 1876. Graduate work in Austria and Germany; practised Minneapolis, Minnesota, 1881-1931. Professor in University of Minnesota Medical College from its founding until made emeritus in 1916. State Senator, 1891-1895. Member of Minneapolis Charter Commission.

Gaston Boyd, M.D., Ohio Medical College, 1873; practised in Illinois and in Newton, Kansas.

Erastus Robinson, born February 26, 1853; died March 10, 1940. M.D., Miami Medical College, 1876. Practised Trenton, Ohio, and Osgood, Indiana.

David Milholland (1858——?—). M.D., Miami Medical College, 1884. Practised at Junction, Paulding County, almost all of his fifty years.

Orsini Scheel, born December 25, 1857. M.D., Ohio Medical College. Practised Hamilton, Ohio. Died February 6, 1941.

Benton Halstead Scott (1860-1927). M.D., Ohio Medical College. Practised Okeana, Ohio; Chicago, Illinois, and Harrison, Ohio.

O. P. McHenry, born New Haven, 1861. M.D., Eclectic Medical College, 1886. Practised Hamilton, Ohio, 1895. Butler County coroner two terms.

Albert Evans, born March 7, 1859. M.D., Ohio Medical College. Practised Cincinnati; house physician Waldorf-Astoria Hotel, New York; practiced London, England, and Chicago, Illinois. Died August 28, 1902.

Minor Morris, born August 23, 1863. Marietta, 1884. M.D., Ohio Medical College. Practised Indianapolis, Indiana. Surgeon First World War. In Army and Navy Medical Museum, Washington, D. C. Practised Alliance, Nebraska. Died March 22, 1926.

John Francis, born February 15, 1862. Wooster, 1886. M.D., Miami Medical College, 1889. Practised Hamilton, Ohio, fifty years. Retired.

J. Frank George, born September 29, 1866. M.D., Ohio Medical College, 1894. Practised Okeana, Ohio, June, 1894, until his death, October, 1921.

SONS AND DAUGHTERS OF THE COMMUNITY 95

Edward Francis, born March 27, 1872. Ohio State University, 1894. M.D., Miami Medical College. Surgeon, U. S. Public Health Service, 1900-1937. Retired.

William F. Jones, born May 23, 1874, Chester Crossroads, now a part of Shaker Heights, Geauga County, Ohio. M.D., Miami Medical College, 1900. See D.V.M.

Burkert Clark. M.D., Miami Medical College, 1901; Christ Hospital, 1902; practised Norwood, Ohio, 1903-1913. Member U. S. Medical Corps, World War I; Shandon, Ohio, 1913 until his death, 1939.

Owen P. Davies (1880-1944). Graduated from American School of Osteopathy, 1910. Practised Punxsutawney, Pennsylvania, 1911-1923; St. Petersburg, Florida, 1923 until his death.

Charles R. Campbell. M.D., Eclectic Medical College, 1906. Practised Newtown, Cincinnati, Ohio. President Hamilton County School Board, 1920.

Joseph E. Pottenger, born April 5, 1878. M.D., University of Southern California, 1905; A.B., 1906. Assistant medical director and director of laboratories, Pottenger Sanatarium for diseases of the chest, Monrovia, California.

Leslie J. Schradin, born November 12, 1900. Miami, 1923; M.D., Cincinnati, 1927. Practised Wyoming, Ohio; also in the employ of Palm Olive Company in South America.

James Appleton, born 1920. Miami, 1943. At present in medical education in Louisville in connection with war service.

DOCTOR OF DENTAL SURGERY

John Marshal Scott, born Crown Point, Indiana, September 5, 1869. Studied under Dr. H. C. Howells of Hamilton; D.D.S., Cincinnati Dental College. Practised Hamilton, Ohio; Nashville, Tennessee; and Glasgow, Montana. Died September 22, 1936.

DOCTORS OF VETERINARY MEDICINE

Mark Francis, born March 19, 1863. O. S. U., 1887, the first graduate of the O. S. U. veterinary school. Taught in Texas A. and M. College for nearly fifty years. He made it possible to produce high-grade cattle in the South by immunization against Texas cattle fever. Died June 28, 1936.

Warner B. Scott, D.V.M., University of Toronto, Canada. Practised Middletown and Hamilton, Ohio, and Connersville, Indiana. Died 1931.

William F. Jones, D.V.M., O. S. U., 1896. M.D., Miami Medical College, 1900. Veterinary inspector, Kansas City, Denver, Chicago, and McCook, Nebraska. Practised veterinary medicine in McCook until his death, August 23, 1924.

Clinton H. Sater, D.V.M., O. S. U., 1902. Practising since that date in Hamilton, Ohio.

Stanley W. Brown, D.V.M., O. S. U., 1907. State veterinary examiner, 1914-1915, Hamilton, Ohio.

Carl M. McCoy, D.V.M., Cincinnati, 1909. Veterinarian and government inspector, Omaha, Nebraska.

TEACHERS FROM THE COMMUNITY

William Bebb, 1826-1832. (See Law.)

Evan Davis taught locally 1830-1840, in Hamilton 1840-1869. County examiner, 1840-1869. Davis and Bebb were examined for teaching certificates by Hon. James Shields, graduate of the University of Glasgow.

The Atherton sisters, Naomi, Mary, and Belinda, all taught in the local schools. Mary taught high school in both Paddy's Run and Venice.

Michael Jones taught three years in Ross and three years in Morgan.

Samuel I. McClelland, Miami 1868, was the first principal of the New London Special District. He was County Examiner, 1874-1876. He taught in Monroe, Butler County, many years.

Frank W. Bell, born December 28, 1848; died 1924. Teacher Morgan, Reily, and Ross Townships from 1870 for fourteen years. In Minnesota two years with his brother, Dr. J. W. Bell. In the Madison school, Hamilton, from 1887 until his retirement in 1912. To his regular services he added night school for writing practice and other branches without compensation and without cost to the student. He was deservedly popular.

The Rev. Samuel T. Wilson, Maryville College, 1878. Missionary in Mexico, 1882-1885. He was first professor, then

SONS AND DAUGHTERS OF THE COMMUNITY

dean, then president of Maryville College, Tennessee, from 1901 to 1930, when he retired. Died July 19, 1944. Age 86.

Mary M. Robinson, Glendale Female College, 1869, taught in New London Special District, in Reily Township, in Crosby Township, Hamilton County; in Madison, Wisconsin, and Keithsburg, Illinois. Was also several years with the Cincinnati Commercial Gazette.

Anne Peate, born in Wales, 1854; died Vaughansville, Ohio, 1945. Taught in Paddy's Run and Venice six years and in Lima for seven years.

Oliver Jones, graduate of Wabash College, taught in the schools of Hamilton, Ohio, many years.

Mattie D. Jones taught in and around Paddy's Run for a generation.

Eliza Francis, student at Oberlin, 1886-1889. Taught at Berea, Kentucky, several years. Was the first public school music teacher in the schools of Shandon and other neighboring communities, 1892-1898. She was followed by W. H. Howells.

Stephen R. Williams, Oberlin, 1892; Harvard, 1900. Taught two years in Lima and forty years in the Department of Zoology, Miami University, 1900-1940. Retired.

Mattie Evans, Miami diploma, 1929. Taught in and about Shandon for more than thirty years.

James Bickley, Miami 1897. Principal, New London Special District, 1893-1895; County Examiner, 1897. Died 1897.

J. A. Goshorn, Miami 1898. Principal Shandon and Okeana; superintendent, western part of Butler County until retirement. Died September 1, 1937.

Emma DeArmond Douglass, taught 1890-1898 in Morgan, Reily, and Oxford schools.

Matthew Duvall, taught 1898-1943, his last position being superintendent of schools, Mt. Healthy, Ohio, 1910-1943. Died October 3, 1943.

Stanley Rowland, Miami 1897. Taught Louisville, Kentucky; Los Angeles, California; LaFollette and Pulaski, Tennessee. Principal of the Shandon schools, 1909-1930. Died December 21, 1942.

David Clark, O. S. U. 1905. Superintendent of schools, Fostoria; Salt Lake City, Utah; Kenton, Van Wert, Marsh Foundation in Van Wert County, King's Mills, Ohio. Died 1942.

Lawrence B. Duvall, student at Miami. Taught Morgan, 1902-1903; Venice, 1903-1905; Tylersville, 1905-1907; Hamilton city schools, 1907-1909. Died November 18, 1918.

Edith Morris, Western College, 1904. Taught Cedarville College, Cedarville, Ohio, 1906-1909, and at Normal and Collegiate Institute, Asheville, North Carolina, 1911-1913.

Wilford Sizelove, Miami 1910. Principal Sixth District School, Covington, Kentucky; at present assistant superintendent of schools, Hamilton County, Ohio.

Ella Duvall, student at Miami. Taught Fairfield, 1918-1928; Overpeck, 1928-1936; New Miami, 1936-1944. Died May, 1945.

William Ross Duvall, student at Miami. Taught in Butler County, 1909-1916.

Samuel F. Doelker, Valparaiso 1912. Taught in Ohio schools eleven years; South Dakota, Cresbard, three years; Oldham, five years, and in Chester for the last twenty years.

Albert Volweiler, Miami, 1910; Ph.D., Pennsylvania. Now professor of history, Ohio University, Athens, Ohio.

J. Milton Amiss, Miami 1911. Teacher, Howe, Indiana, 1911-1918; education director, Reo Motor Car Company, 1918. director of industrial education, Dodge Apprentice School, 1943————.

Gordon G. Starr, Wilmington, 1920; A.M., O. S. U. Taught in Manchester High School, 1916-1918. U. S. Navy, 1918-1919. Taught Findlay High School, 1920-1929; superintendent of schools, Arcanum, Ohio, 1929-1942. Dean, 1942-1943, and acting president, 1943-1944, of Pfeiffer Junior College, Misenheimer, North Carolina.

Edna Walther, Miami 1925. At present, Hamilton High School.

Florence Francis, Oberlin (Public School Music), 1918; Miami, 1933. Music supervisor, Shandon and other schools, then Ross school, and 1943, Hamilton schools.

Mabel Evans, elementary schools, Morgan Township, 1911-1920.

SONS AND DAUGHTERS OF THE COMMUNITY

Clayton H. Starr, Wilmington, 1926. Taught Arcanum, 1926-1928; principal of high school, 1928-1942; superintendent of schools, Arcanum, 1942————.

Clara Wilkins Irwin, Earlham, 1923. Taught in high schools in Hamilton and Butler Counties five years.

J. Kenneth Koger, Miami, 1925. School principal, Hamilton; assistant principal, Hamilton High School.

Mary Evans Quinlin, Miami diploma, 1930.

Martha Evans, Miami diploma, 1932.

Dorothy Clawson, Western College, 1937. Middletown Junior High School, 1937————.

Business Men from the Community

Evan R. Bebb, brother of Governor Bebb, born 1804, died 1864. Entered business in New York City. He kept up his family associations and his interest in the Paddy's Run community. He and his business partner, a Mr. Graham, assisted the formation of a second library association in 1852, both by donations of books from their own libraries and by helping to select the books to be purchased by the membership fees. His firm was the immediate predecessor of A. T. Stewart & Company, pioneer department store.

John Evans, born in Wales, 1795; died 1891. Came to Paddy's Run, 1818; married Sarah Nicholas, 1821. He was a natural financier who would have made his mark in any business. As a farmer, starting from the bottom, he was worth $100,000 at the time of his death and had he not in his later years stepped out of his line to deal with city slickers, his fortune would have been much larger. In the hard times following the panic of 1837, having just lost all his hogs by cholera, against the advice of his sons and neighbors, he bought all the pigs he could find in near-by Indiana, fed them and sold them at such a price that he later said: "My mistake then was that I did not buy all the Paddy's Run valley."

He left a monument to his name, the watering trough at the spring on the slope his horse had to ascend each time the family went to the village.

Matthew Russell Shields, son of James Shields, was for some time a school teacher, and for nine years was surveyor of Butler County. He lived his later years in Mt. Carmel, Indiana.

Evan Morris, civil engineer, was educated in the local schools and received his professional training from Professor Ormsby B. Mitchell of Cincinnati, later the founder of the Cincinnati Observatory and a well known astronomer. Mr. Morris was especially active in the road-building period of Ohio, 1835-1860.

John L. Evans, born in Virginia, 1827; died in Shandon, 1895. His father, William Evans (born 1790; died 1843), a soldier in the Napoleonic wars, 1808-1815, and present at the battle of Waterloo, is buried in the old Paddy's Run graveyard. His mother's father was a Revolutionary soldier. They came to Paddy's Run in 1832. John L. Evans married Josephine Price in 1870 and they had two sons, Lloyd Price and Glenn. He kept store in the village all his life, often was postmaster and was the backbone of the opposition to the change of the name of the postoffice through the three attempts from 1857 to 1892.

William S. Manuel, born April 21, 1864; died June 6, 1919. Went to Cleveland in 1897 to work for his uncle, J. Sutphin Jones. He developed a lake shipping business of his own and when it became too large to handle alone sent for his brother, John (born June 14, 1873, died February 2, 1940). The firm, W. S. and J. S. Manuel, is still doing business in the Rockefeller Building, Cleveland.

Supply Butterfield, born 1866, died 1939. He drove the Paddy's Run-Cincinnati bus a year or so in the eighties, was a prominent Democrat, and was for twenty years on the Hamilton County Board of Elections.

Thomas J. J. Scheel, born January 8, 1867, died May 24, 1945, was a grocer and for thirty-nine years director and treasurer of the Eagle Savings and Loan Company in Cincinnati.

John Guthrie, born 1868. Postmaster at Shandon for thirty-one years; appointed during the administration of Theodore Roosevelt; retired for age, 1940.

SONS AND DAUGHTERS OF THE COMMUNITY

William Atherton, born 1869, died 1939. Established a successful wholesale and retail grocery and fruit store on Court Street, Hamilton, which is still known as the Atherton market.

Hugh Williams Clark, born December 24, 1869, died October 15, 1940. He spent his childhood in Paddy's Run and studied at Oberlin, 1887-1891. In office work in New York City, 1897-1900. He was a clerk in the office of the Brotherhood of Railway Engineers in Cleveland from 1900-1938, when he retired for age.

Charles Scheel, born 1876, died 1941. Machinist with Procter and Gamble, Staten Island, New York.

Minor Evans, born May 16, 1872, died June 6, 1925. Hamilton, Ohio, superintendent of Butler County Infirmary, March 1, 1911, to March 1, 1913; connected with a Lima, Ohio, bakery, May, 1913-April, 1919; in coal business, May, 1919, to his death.

John D. Evans, Jr. Business, St. Louis, Missouri.

James Scott, born February 27, 1872. Farm machinery salesman, ranchman in Arizona, retired and living in St. Petersburg, Florida.

Clarence DeArmond, born 1872, died 1917. Bought a hotel on Second Street, Hamilton, in 1912 and gave it his name. It started successfully on the European plan catering to travelling men. Soon three floors of a near-by building had to be taken for an annex. In the flood of 1913 the cellars and ground floors were filled with silt. Mr. DeArmond's health failing, he transferred the hotel to other management, and developed a successful real estate subdivision in College Hill.

William Vaughan Evans, born June 5, 1882; family moved to Kingston, Indiana. In business in Chicago, 1910————.

Charles E. Starlin, Miami 1902. Chemist with Procter and Gamble, Staten Island, New York, until his death, April 1, 1934.

C. Kirby Robinson, born January 1, 1883; died August 12, 1914. Miami 1904. In automobile business, Seattle, Washington.

W. Ernest Scott, born July 26, 1880. Marietta 1904. With Whitaker Paper Company, Chicago.

Lillian Woodruff, deputy in office of Probate Court, Hamilton, Ohio, from 1904.

Earl F. Colborn, born June 15, 1886. Miami, 1907; A.M., University of Cincinnati. Professor of history, Miami, 1910-1914. Agent, Connecticut Mutual Life, 1915 to date. Major in Army Air Force, 1943. Service in India.

Paul Robinson, born April 22, 1885. Miami 1907. Funeral director, Shandon.

W. Ross DeArmond, born October 22, 1887. Student at Miami, 1904-1906. With Farm Bureau Insurance, Columbus, Ohio.

Benjamin Chidlaw Morris, born February 29, 1888. Miami 1909. Manager Whitaker Paper Company, Indianapolis and Detroit, now with Vegetable Parchment Paper Company, Kalamazoo, Michigan. In 1943, a dollar-a-year man in Washington, allocating wood pulp to paper mills.

Hally Mering Scott, born January 28, 1889. Oberlin, 1911; A.M., University of Missouri, 1914. Signal Corps U. S. Army, 1917-1919. Geologist, Riverland Oil Company, Tulsa, Oklahoma, 1919————.

Paul Teetor, born July 11, 1888. Miami, 1909; M.A., Illinois, 1911. Ceramic engineer. Member faculty, University of Kansas, 1914-1917; ceramist, Staso Manufacturing Company, Poultney, Vermont.

Stanley Schradin. With Ford Motor Company, Seattle, Washington.

Roland D. Francis, born June 30, 1903. Miami 1925. With Procter and Gamble since 1925; assistant treasurer, 1942; manager, tax division, 1943————.

Edward Wilds. Cashier, Farmer's State Bank, Miamitown, Ohio.

Writers

Two nationally known journalists have come from Paddy's Run—Murat Halstead, war correspondent and editor, and Albert Shaw, editor and author.

Another newspaperman, born "on Paddy" about 1860, was Henry James, whose family moved to Iowa when he was a small child. He was a newspaperman for fifty years, reporting on the Rocky Mountain News, Omaha Herald, San Francisco

SONS AND DAUGHTERS OF THE COMMUNITY 103

Examiner, and Pasadena Post. He also served at one time as publicity chief for the Union Pacific Railroad. He died in Pasadena, California, in November, 1933.

Alice Cary Reese, who lived all of her life in the Paddy's Run valley, wrote a book illustrating the characteristics of a Welsh colony and the changes as it became Americanized, "Hurrah for America," published in 1898. This story is based on personal incidents and reminiscences. Miss Reese attended Western Female Academy in 1869-1871, but did not complete her work there as she was injured in the fire of 1871.

Mrs. Robert S. Mann (Helen Josephine Scott), a grandniece of Murat Halstead, and a graduate of Miami University, has served in various editorial positions and has been a member of the journalism faculties of the University of Missouri and New York University.

CHAPTER XIV

SPECIAL BIOGRAPHIES

JAMES NICHOLAS, Sr., was evidently a man of independent mind, for during the process of being educated for the ministry of the English Established Church, he chose to give it up and live a pioneer life in the new country across the sea.

His descendants report him a good mathematician and a fine penman as evidenced by his diary. He also left a sketchbook of the drawings he had made in Wales and a combination text of grammar and geography, brought over when he came in 1794.

He and his wife, Mary Morris Nicholas, of Carmarthenshire, left Liverpool in March and landed in Philadelphia on May 11, 1794, Mrs. Nicholas' twentieth birthday. They made their way to Beulah, Cambria County, and there he became a blacksmith and learned to repair the mechanisms used in those early days.

Preparing to leave Beulah for farther west, he made use of his training in iron and wood working and built a small boat for the transport of his wife, his 2-year-old daughter Martha and himself into the wilderness. The boat was launched in the Conemaugh near where Johnstown now is and in two weeks of travel by day they traversed the Conemaugh, the Kiskimetas and the Allegheny to Pittsburgh. The next 500 miles to Cincinnati was by flatboat and must have been much less nerve wracking than traveling alone in a rowboat.

Mr. Nicholas was the first blacksmith to settle on the Paddy's Run. Chidlaw says the Nicholas family arrived in 1803 and we know that John Vaughan, who bought from the government in 1802, sold 100 acres of the south end of the east half of section 25, Morgan Township, to Mr. Nicholas.

The Paddy's Run goes through this farm and there he constructed a sawmill of the sash type and is said to have impounded the spring flood water so that the mill could run a good share of the year. (A second sawmill was located further up the Run by the Parkinsons; it had less water and a shorter working time.)

His son, James, Jr., one of the three founders of Gomer, Allen County, left in 1833, Mr. Nicholas and his wife following the next year. Mr. Nicholas died within a few months and his was one of the first burials in Pike Run cemetery. Mrs. Nicholas returned to Paddy's Run to live with her daughter, Sarah, and son-in-law, John Evans. She died in 1861 at 87 and is buried in the old graveyard.

(The foregoing was taken in part from a letter by David Nicholas, written in 1915.)

The following sketch of Roger Williams (1850-1873) was written by Dr. Albert Shaw:

"I wish to tell of the most brilliant and influential student at Miami University whom I have ever known. Roger Williams, 1872, was in his day the shining light of Miami. He excelled in everything that he tried. He was seven years my senior and I followed him slavishly.

"Those were the great early days of baseball and he was the captain of the Miami team and leader in all the athletic life of the institution. He was unapproached in his record as a student, and especially brilliant in languages and history. He had decided upon a career of journalism and for several years he was editor of the Miami Student and often wrote the greater part of the paper. Looking to his future work, he bought the local weekly paper, the Oxford Citizen, with its printing office and it was there that I first blackened my fingers with the printer's ink that, figuratively speaking, has never been wholly removed for more than fifty years.

"Roger was the son of a prosperous farmer in our village. He was clear-headed and determined and would not play the role of an awkward country boy but shared with a nephew of General Schenck the distinction of being the most fastidious of all students in dress and manner.

"Under President Hepburn's advice, in 1872-1873 he went to Germany for graduate study and in one week of intensive study of German under a skillful teacher, prepared himself for taking notes from his German professors.

"During the summer vacation after his junior year he performed the great task of compiling the national catalogue of Beta Theta Pi, the first of the national fraternities founded at Miami. I spent that summer as his assistant in the work of listing and cataloguing. That I and my two sons happen now to be Betas is largely due to the sentiment surviving from those associations.

"Through all his college years Roger Williams was the responsible leader of the younger life of our neighborhood. He consulted with our teachers and advised us in our reading and our methods of study. He died at twenty-three, but his influence had been formative in the lives of not a few of his younger neighbors and proteges."

Will T. Lewis was the first man to volunteer at the Paddy's Run meeting in April, 1861, after President Lincoln's call for 75,000 men. The next Sunday evening the Butler County volunteers met in Beckett's Hall, Hamilton, on their way to Columbus. Mrs. Davidson, wife of the United Presbyterian pastor, saw a boyish looking young fellow standing alone. To her question he said he was a stranger and an orphan, and she offered to be his mother for the duration of the war and to follow him with her prayers.

In a letter dated June 23, 1862, written to Abner Francis, there appears the following: "P. S. Know all men by these presents that Col. W. H. H. Taylor did on or about the tenth day of June, '62, appropriate for his own use one box, sent by friends from Paddy's Run to soldier friends.

"Very Respectfully, Will T. Lewis,

"Co. H, Third Battalion, 5th O.V.C., Corinth, Mississippi."

Toward the latter part of the war Lewis was made a First Lieutenant and Adjutant of the U. S. 110th regiment of colored troops and served to the end of the war.

After the war he started to prepare for law, but it went against the grain. In 1872 he was ordained as a Methodist minister by the West Virginia Conference; served in the Northern Ohio Conference, 1878-1884; was in St. Louis, 1885-

1893; Arkansas, 1894-1896; Troy, Ohio, 1896-1901; at Mt. Pleasant Church, Wilmington, Delaware, 1901-1903; Oxford, Maryland, 1904-1907; St. George's, Delaware, 1908; and at Oxford, Maryland, again in 1909. He went to the Wyoming, Pennsylvania, Conference in 1910, and no later information has been obtained.

Mr. Lewis returned to Paddy's Run as Decoration Day orator in 1889, an occasion described by Mrs. Annie Chidlaw Morris as follows:

"The old soldiers, twenty in number, were the heroes of the day. David Francis gave a history of what Morgan Township did during the war and the part taken by those who remained at home.

"Minter C. Morris sang 'The Sword of Bunker Hill.' Orsini Scheel and Rev. Hugh Scott gave brief addresses and then the orator of the day spoke a full hour and was listened to with great interest. He was a Methodist minister from St. Louis, Rev. Will T. Lewis. He was clerking in Robinson's store when the war broke out and was the first to enlist from the village. He came at his own expense for the sake of old memories.

"The wreaths were carried to the graves, sixteen in number, by the veterans, accompanied by the band. The rain interfered with the plan of the young ladies carrying the flowers."

Honoring eight soldiers from Paddy's Run was a cross of white roses on a green and white pyramid, with the inscription,

"In loving memorial of the soldiers of the republic from Morgan Township. Their bodies lie buried in the Southland."

Names of the eight are: Josiah Dean, Wilson Mercer, John H. Morris, John Fenton, Thomas Thomas, A. Martindale, David Ross, and Harry T. Scott.

At one time when the Paddy's Run church was without a pastor, Lyman Beecher was asked to preach. He drove out the twenty-five miles from Cincinnati on Saturday afternoon and when his horse and buggy were being put away it was noted that there was a package under the seat. When he came in to supper, the man who had seen the package asked the

SPECIAL BIOGRAPHIES

minister if he should bring it in with his carpetbag. Mr. Beecher jumped up and gasped, "Why, that must be the roast I bought for Mrs. Beecher's dinner tomorrow."

Benton Halstead was the son of Col. Griffin Halstead and the younger brother of Murat Halstead. He was born March 11, 1834, was graduated from Farmers College and read law. He enlisted in 1861 in the 69th Ohio Volunteer Infantry and was appointed Sergeant Major. In 1862 he was discharged to join the 79th regiment as Major. He was wounded at Resaca, was in the battles of Lookout Mountain, Peach Tree Hill, and the siege of Atlanta. He served on General Sherman's staff on the March to the Sea. At the end of the war he was appointed Brevet Colonel.

He practiced law in Cincinnati for a number of years and later was an attorney in the Pension Office in Washington. He died in Washington December 26, 1919, and was buried with military honors in Arlington National Cemetery.

His son, Laurence Halstead, a graduate of West Point Military Academy, served in the Philippines in the Spanish War and in World War I, became a Brigadier General in 1931. He was then Office Chief of Infantry, Washington, D. C. He is now retired.

His grandson, Mervin Halstead, a graduate of Annapolis, 1931, a Lieutenant Commander in the Navy (1944), is in active service in World War II.

Daniel Woodruff, as a 10-year-old, witnessed the Battle of Bunker Hill, and as one of the retiring colonial soldiers passed, the boy was handed a musket which is still preserved in the family. He moved to Pennsylvania and then to Ohio in early life. Some of his children were born in Butler County.

His son, Reuben, was the first to suffer from cholera in the epidemic of 1834 and his grandson, John, the first to die in that epidemic.

Daniel Woodruff's daughter Sarah married a soldier and pioneer and became an early settler in Tennessee. I have been unable to learn the name of her husband, who died, leaving her with two children. About this time David Crockett's first wife died, leaving him with two young children, and, to quote Crockett, "We decided to join forces."

After the death of Crockett in the Alamo in 1837 and the growing up of both sets of children, from time to time "Aunt Sally" Crockett visited her brother Reuben in Morgan Township, and her nieces and nephews had many stories to tell to their children of their jolly aunt.

James T. Patton, a veteran of two wars, died July 30, 1922, at the age of 92. He had lived in the community for sixty years. He was toll-gate keeper, cobbler, general repair man, and janitor.

He was a unique character in many ways and as the conscientious janitor of the Congregational Church he touched more lives in his humble way than most people are able to. Many of us recall his squeaky Sunday shoes, said by the small boys to be alligator hide, and his habitual practice in cold weather of poking up the fires in the two big cannon stoves during the singing of the first hymn of the evening service.

With her aunt, Ann Morgan, Eliza Evans came from Wales about 1850. The two young women found places in domestic service in Cincinnati and made acquaintances in Paddy's Run. Ann Morgan married David E. Davies, son of the Evan Davies named in Morgan Gwilym's 1818 letter to his brother which appears earlier in this history. Mrs. Davies died, leaving her husband with two young sons, so Eliza dropped her work in Cincinnati to come out and care for the family. She stayed till the boys were grown. Those who knew David E. were familiar with his tenacity of purpose, or stubbornness, as Eliza termed it. However, according to the boys, she almost always won the disputed point, since if she threatened to return to Cincinnati he always capitulated, saying "Don't leave us, Eliza, don't leave us." When at last she returned to Cincinnati, she kept house for a minister and his family for many years and loved them as if they were her very own.

Job Woolley came to the village in 1834 and had a tavern on the Millville road opposite the spot where the new church was built later. He had a stage line which ran intermittently between points in Indiana and Cincinnati. The sign in front of his tavern was a large barrel-head elevated on a post with a horse's head painted on the north side and a mule's head on the south to indicate that all were welcome inside.

SPECIAL BIOGRAPHIES

Pat and Owen were making the rounds one Saturday night and the two Celts, Irish and Welsh, stopped, one on each side of the sign.

"'Tis a foine mule," says Pat.

"Hee," says Owen, deant ye know a horse-head wen ye see him?" And both started a barrage of fists. Occupants of the saloon piled out, grabbed both fighters and dragged them inside to treat and be treated. After some time the two emerged, sworn friends, and said Pat, looking up at the short ears of the creature on his side of the sign, "Begorra, Ownie, ye was right. I 'pologize, it's a harse."

On his side, Owen, seeing the jackrabbit-like ears, thought that Pat was poking fun at him, so he took a poke at Pat and the fight was on again, though by this time neither was sufficiently himself to damage the other and friends were able to steer each to a place where he could sleep off his fighting spirit(s).

Bill and Dave Lewis lived along the Millville road about two and a half miles north of the village. Dave was the older, but Bill had caught up with him in height and was a little heavier. The boys were going to Sunday school in rather dilapidated clothes, so Mrs. Lewis bought a roll of blue jeans to make a suit for each. She was an experienced seamstress, but there wasn't enough free time in a week to make more than one suit. So on Sunday she told Dave to put on the new suit and Bill to go as he had been going, promising him a new suit the next Sunday.

The nearest path to the village led over the hill and through the woods out of sight of home. When the woods were reached Bill ordered Dave to change clothes or take a licking such as Bill could give him. So the boys went to Sunday school, new suit on Bill, old one on Dave, and on the return trip the shift was made again and again Dave was threatened with a licking if he said a word at home about the transaction.

As far as I know there were two suits for the boys the next Sunday, but the story came out as some one not in the secret complimented Mrs. Lewis on her handiwork on Bill's suit.

Miami University's annual commencement on June 11, 1929, was really a "Shandon" commencement, or at any rate, the community felt that way about it when Miami gave honorary degrees to Albert Shaw, the commencement speaker, founder of the American Review of Reviews and its editor for forty-six years; to Mark Francis, who introduced an immunizing process against the ravages of Texas fever by which pure-bred beef and milk breeds of cattle were able to supplant the native scrubs and scrawny longhorns of the Southwest; to Edward Francis, scientist, best known for his study of tularemia (rabbit fever), a new disease of man; and to Lowry F. Sater, distinguished lawyer and political leader in Ohio.

Unfortunately Dr. Shaw was convalescing from a serious illness and was unable to be present. His son, Roger, read his address, from which is taken the eulogy of Roger Williams found in this history.

The whole Shandon community, both those resident and those who had gone out from it over the United States, were saying: "I knew him when . . ." and "He certainly has done well for us."

"Politics held little interest for the settlers in Paddy's Run until the year 1824, chiefly remembered for the vigorous political campaign between John Quincy Adams and Andrew Jackson," Roger Williams wrote in 1871. "Previous to this time scarcely any interest had been shown throughout the neighborhood in politics, many of the immigrants had neglected to secure naturalization papers, but in this year excitement ran high and the politics of the community became for the first time distinctly defined. The pioneers were for Jackson and voted the Democratic ticket for his successor. In the year 1840 the Liberty (Free Soil) party took its rise and its first convert in the neighborhood was Hugh Williams, who cast the only ticket in the election of 1844 for Birney. The following year Hezekiah Shaw and Moses Marsh voted that ticket. By degrees the party grew until in the election of Buchanan, although the township went Democratic the neighborhood was Republican." (From the manuscript of Roger Williams, 1871.)

CHAPTER XV

THE OLD GRAVEYARD AND THE CHURCHES

The Old Graveyard
by S. R. Williams and Annie F. Crafts

ON OCTOBER 6, 7, and 8, 1942, my cousin Annie Francis Crafts and I made a census and an approximate diagram of the graves in the old burying ground by the community house in Shandon. This plot was given by John Vaughan and Morgan Gwilym along the line between their farms about 1825, and was in use until 1870, when the larger cemetery west of the village took its place. This first community cemetery followed and replaced a number of private burying grounds on individual farms.

The system on which the graves were arranged is not consistent and is hard to follow. Since the Paddy's Run valley is underlaid to a certain extent with quick-sand, some of the early monuments are horizontal slabs of sandstone or granite supported on a brick foundation. Some of these brick foundations are badly broken down and very likely the perfect ones are those which have been repaired. Many of the marble slabs are down. The work of water, frost, and air for over a century first loosened them from their bases and the storm winds from one direction or another completed the work. Some of them broke as they fell. (Feasible repair would seem to be to prepare a concrete base and imbed the broken pieces on the base at such a slant that water will drain off and you would have a grave marker very like the old horizontal tomb and about as permanent.)

No one of these memorials is equal to the present day granite monument which, judging by the best of our glacial boulders, should last ten thousand years, by which time our cemeteries will probably be transformed into fields for the production of food.

We found a number of stones illegible. Many of the others needed to have the lettering cleaned, but by using a trowel and a wire brush where necessary we were able to get 285 names. There are likely many unmarked graves also; so there were probably more than 300 burials in the plot, approximately 140 by 200 feet. The northeast corner has few gravestones in it.

The ages at death as recorded on tombstones have been arranged by decades and shown in comparison with mortality statistics in the United States based on the 1930 census.

Age years	Sex not given	Male	Female	Percent	U. S. Percent
0- 9	34	34	37	36.8	13.9
10-19		18	10	9.8	3.3
20-29		13	16	*10.2	5.76
30-39		10	13	8.1	7.03
40-49		9	10	6.7	9.9
50-59		6	5	3.8	*13.57
60-69		16	15	10.9	17.4
70-79		11	13	8.4	18.66
80-89		5	10	5.3	9.81
90-99		—	—	—	1.5
100-109		—	—	—	.09

285 burials 1825-1869

Percentage of deaths in each age group per thousand deaths recorded in the registration group of the U. S. for the decade which ended 1930.

The middle of the graveyard group falls somewhere in the third decade. (The ages have not been averaged, but the average would be under 30 years.) The oldest woman, Elizabeth Appleton, aged 89 years, 9 months and 17 days, and the oldest man, George Mering, aged 87 years, 7 months and 27 days, probably lived more years than all of the 87 who died in the first five years of the first decade.

The smaller number of deaths in the 40-59 decades is no doubt due to the fact that Paddy's Run was a distributing point on the way from Wales to daughter settlements such as Gomer, Vaughnsville, Venedocia in northern Ohio, the Fort Wayne region in Indiana, and even Iowa and Kansas. The older members of a family usually moved with, or followed their adventuring children and hence were buried in the younger settlement.

THE OLD GRAVEYARD AND THE CHURCHES 115

The numbers in these two sets of figures—ages at death as recorded in the Paddy's Run graveyard and the deaths by decades per thousand deaths of the 1930 census—were reduced to percentages. When the two diagrams are plotted on one base, the Paddy's Run data make a curve skewed strongly to the left and the mortality statistics curve is as distinctly skewed to the right with its median point high up in the 50-59 decade. We can consider Paddy's Run as representative of the general health condition which persisted through historic times and the 1930 statistics as the result of the knowledge of germs and the correlated hygienic practices developed in the last 80 years.

Here in the Miami Valley, a garden spot of the world, no pioneer farmer ever needed to go hungry. Large families were an asset. There was abundant food most of the year with a danger of too much "hog and hominy" in the winter. Though the early settlers had never heard of vitamins, I am sure they had an ample supply. Unfortunately, refrigeration had not yet reached beyond the stage of a spring house for keeping the milk cool, and even doctors did not conceive of the dangers of the as yet unknown microbes. Malaria (bad air) was as near as they could come to the cause of the omnipresent chills and fever, and when there came a pestilence, as in 1834 when the Asiatic cholera came, they sat up with the patient, drank from the same gourd or tin dipper and died in the same way "by the inscrutable workings of Providence."

No wonder that the greatest number of deaths among these 285 were those of infants less than a year old and that 37 per cent of the whole were children of 9 years or less. Our old people live little longer than these—there are 15 of the 285 who were 80 years or older. Our families are much smaller than theirs, but with modern knowledge of germs and the skill of doctors, a much higher per cent of the children is saved to grow up and die of cancer, heart disease and what-you-will in the years of life beyond 60.

There are 62 surnames found on the tombstones in the old cemetery. Repetition of Jones, Evans, Bebb, Williams, Morgan, Morris, Vaughan, Davies and Griffith indicates that 60 per cent of those buried there are persons of Welsh origin although more than half the surnames are English, French, German from the older colonies. The table which follows shows the names with a numeral giving the frequency of repetition.

Surnames Found in the Graveyard

Name	#	Name	#	Name	#
Anderson	1	Hidlay	4	Phyllis	1
Appleton	7	Hogarth	1	Powell	2
Atherton	3	Humphreys	2	Reese	2
Bebb	13	Ingham	2	Robison	2
Boldridge	1	James	2	Roberts	2
Brown	7	Jones	38	Sater	2
Brundage	1	Kibbe	1	Shaw	1
Bunnel	1	Lewis	5	Shields	5
Carter	2	Lloyd	3	Smith	3
Chidlaw	4	Lyle	1	Starlin	1
Davies	8	McBride	2	Swancott	1
Davis	5	McClelland	4	Thomas	1
Dearmond	14	Mering	8	Tull	3
Ellis	2	Milholland	2	Vanausdall	2
Erven	1	Morgan	12	Vaughan	9
Evans	22	Morris	12	Waer	1
Fisher	1	Mullen	2	Wilkins	6
Francis	3	Nicholas	1	Williams	13
Griffiths	6	Otto	1	Wynn	1
Gwilym	5	Owens	3	Youmans	4
Harris	1	Paul	1		

One unusually slender marble slab, with a glass-covered daguerreotype set in a socket near the top, was the delight of our childhood to spell out. Alas, it has fallen and is broken into three or four sections and is not now readable. It used to read:

Gone to Rest

MARY ADALINE

daughter of Michael and Julia

WILKINS

Died Dec. 27 1858 aged 9 years 7 mos. and 3 days. She could sing and play upwards of 40 tunes on her dulcimer and had played correctly for two years past, but our dearly beloved child was called to that choir which knows no discord and whose melody is Eternal.

> Dear little Adda, how short was thy stay,
> How soon Death has called thy bright spirit away.
> How soon has the tie which thy innocence wove
> Been broken on earth to be united above.

How fondly we watched thee day after day
And loved to behold thee in innocence play.
What bright hopes we cherished but alas they were vain
For we never on earth can caress thee again.
Oh dear little Adda must we bid thee goodbye
And leave thee 'neath the clods of the valley to lie?
Oh, we cannot forget thee, our dearly loved child,
Though flowers may bloom and nature may smile.
Those bright little eyes are now closed from the day,
That fair little form must now moulder away,
But the angelic spirit of Adda, our girl
Now basks in the sunshine of heavenly joy.

The Old Welsh Church Building, 1825-1924
by Edith Morris

Just across the fence from the graveyard stands the old Welsh Church building, now the community house. The brick were burned in 1823 and the foundation, 43 by 30 feet, was laid. The next year the walls were erected and the building enclosed, and in 1825 temporary seats and a pulpit made of two uprights and a board, furnished the house. Thirty years later the congregation had so grown that a new place of worship was built and the old building became a utility building.

Varied indeed have been the uses made of the "old church," the most far-reaching and significant a Select School until the New London Special School District, set apart by legislative action, put up its own school building.

It housed a series of singing schools conducted by different leaders: Mr. Churchill of Oxford, 1848-1855; Mr. Oldfather of Oxford, 1869; Mr. William Black of Okeana, 1882-1883; and Mr. C. C. Case of Oberlin.

In the days when legal difficulties were tried before the justice of the peace, court was held in this building by Squire Benny Lyle and others.

Literary societies flourished here and died and were revived again. Debates filled the house to its capacity, the name of the postoffice was three times argued about pro and con, and discussion often grew interesting in Free Silver days. Entertainments of all kinds, concerts, theatricals, ice cream and strawberry suppers date back to early days and great pride was taken in vying with one's neighbor at the poultry show.

Perhaps nothing of more value and real pleasure than the Loan Exhibition, 1902 (or the station on the Antique Tour later) was ever held there. These were displays of interesting and unique things possessed in the community—beautiful coverlets, the equipment for spinning, rare dishes and cooking utensils, farming implements, ancient money, ancestral firearms, rare books, pictures, tester and trundle beds, and other things accumulated in a hundred years which illustrate more history than many pages could tell.

The plans for remodeling the old church had just matured when we entered the first World War, and all building, of course, stopped. At its close the project was resumed. It was the aim of the building committee to construct as much of a building as could be paid for reasonably, without imposing on the community a debt which would be a burden for years. The post-war price of materials was almost prohibitive, the wages of hired labor equally prohibitive. For these reasons, work progressed slowly, for much of it was done by voluntary labor of men of the community.

The structure, 43 by 30 feet, remains intact as it stood through the years—in good condition. In front of this original building, which is the auditorium, was constructed, beginning at the east, a light, convenient kitchen; opening from it to the west, a spacious room which may be used for a dining room or thrown into the main auditorium for large audiences; on the west end of this room is an entry 10 by 22 feet opening into the auditorium and also into the dining room. The finished basement contains a hot-air furnace which heats the entire building which is lighted from the village electric light plant.

Every thoughtful person can realize the important place this building occupies in the life of the community, the ideal community center under the control and supervision of the church, where can be held concerts, plays, quiltings, club meetings, Farm Bureau meetings, Farmers' Institutes—everything that is wholesome and advisable for the community.

THE OLD GRAVEYARD AND THE CHURCHES

Churches

In the later part of the nineteenth century German families, both Protestant and Catholic, came into the Paddy's Run region and naturally planned churches for their peoples.

In 1873 or 1874 a number of the Catholic families of the community began to consider establishing a church, according to information furnished by Thomas J. J. Scheel. They must have met together in the different homes from time to time. A lot was purchased in the middle of the village and the house on it moved over to the cemetery road.

The leaders in this enterprise were Jacob Scheel, Benedict Pfeffer, Laurence Braun, Peter Knauss, Sr., Mrs. John Straub, the Hines family of near Scipio, Laurence Miller, George Baker, Michael Schaefer, Tom Kinney and Thaddeus Sonnentag.

In 1878 St. Aloysius Church, a building 30 by 60 feet, seating 300, was completed. Many contributions of money and materials came from Hamilton and other places, all the hauling being done by local members.

This building burned in 1900, but since the walls were little damaged, it was at once rebuilt and regular services continue to the present under the ministration of Father Bernard Gerbus, O.F.M.

History of tke United Brethren Church
by Ruth Walther Wilson and Edna Walther

The United Brethren held services first in the old Welsh Church, now the community house. Among the leaders in this organization were John and Fred Walther, Jacob and Killian Doelker, John and Mathias Scheering.

Their United Brethren circuit was made up of four churches, Harrison, New Baltimore, and Paddy's Run in Ohio and Trenton in Indiana. Services were held every Sunday; every three months a quarterly meeting was held at one of the four churches in sequence. Also each church took its turn, yearly, as the host church for two weeks of protracted meetings (revivals) in the winter.

120 THE SAGA OF THE PADDY'S RUN

The Rev. Valentine Assel was the pastor when the church at Shandon was erected in 1886 and later he was followed by his son, the Rev. John Assel.

The building, on land owned by John Walther, was erected by John Pfotzer (still living in 1943, aged 94) of Harrison, John Little and Page Sortwell of Lawrenceburg, with Henry Reiser and John Scheidt as helpers. The structure was complete in a little more than a month.

The congregation came from many parts of Germany and the German language was used in the church through its entire existence. As the younger generation preferred services in English and the older people became fewer and less influential, the church gradually disbanded. Some of the members joined a United Brethren church at New Haven, some did not affiliate with any other organization and some joined the Congregational Church in the village, which fifty years earlier had gone through a similar language difficulty as the pioneer Welsh dropped off.

HISTORY OF THE CONGREGATIONAL CHURCH FROM 1856

by Clara Francis

(For the early history of the church community see Appendix II and III)

The first building 30 feet by 43 feet, was erected on land given by John Vaughan and Morgan Gwilym for both church and graveyard. When in 1853 the building needed modification, the committee decided to secure a larger lot and build a more central building. An acre of ground, facing on both roads, was purchased and a rectangular building of New England pattern, 40 feet by 60 feet, was started. A serious accident, the collapse of the steeple, killed or fatally injured six men (see Appendix III) and the church was boarded up and left unfinished till 1856.

The interior of the building had a plain auditorium with a single row of pews on either side and aisles separating these from the double row of pews in the center. On the north wall (front) of the room two pillars, one on each side of the platform, extended nearly to the ceiling and supported a carved beam. There were steps from the aisle on either side to the platform, and wood posts, each bearing a lamp, stood at the top of the steps. In each corner were pews facing the minister's desk for the choir and the church officers. From the center of the ceiling hung a chandelier holding a number of kerosene lamps. Others were on the walls. Two large soft-coal stoves heated the room. At the back, over the vestibule and the small rooms on either side, was a balcony for the overflow audience at large meetings.

When in 1865 a clear-toned bell of 600 pounds weight was hung in the steeple the community felt its church was completed.

An organ was purchased in 1871. Later, in the pastorate of the Rev. C. A. Gleason, the corner pews were removed and the platform extended to the west wall to afford space for choir and organ on the higher level.

Until 1884 the pastors lived in rented houses or in homes of their own. (The house built by B. W. Chidlaw about 1840 stands in perfect condition.) In that year, 1884, the church purchased half an acre of land facing the Brookville pike and erected a manse for the minister at a cost of $2,235. Gifts and legacies amounting to $450 were applied on the cost of this project.

In the winter of 1902, looking toward the coming centennial of the church, an Old Relic Show was staged in the old church and it was a memorable event, calling out the things of a forgotten generation, and fixing the minds of the people on the coming anniversary. Before the time for the centennial the church had the kerosene lamps replaced by a gasoline lighting system, the interior was redecorated and a new fence placed around the yard.

August 26 and 27, 1903, were the dates set for the centennial gathering and as many former residents as were able returned for the two-day reunion. Murat Halstead and Albert Shaw, eminent sons of the community, were on the program and the final oration, "The Influence of Early Settlers Upon the Character of the Community," given by President William Oxley Thompson of Ohio State University, was a fitting climax to a celebration which filled the descendants of these settlers with honest pride.

Eight years later, in 1911, the choir and a number of the older men and women practiced the old songs they had learned in the earlier singing schools. This group, appearing in the costumes of a by-gone day, gave a concert to a church filled to capacity. Since it was such a success, the troupe repeated the performance in several near-by communities, turning the proceeds over to the church repair fund.

In the fall and winter of 1911-1912, under the leadership of the Rev. Jacob Hawk of Cincinnati, the Sunday School increased in membership and in addition a large class of men was enrolled. So when the Rev. S. D. Wellwood took up the pastorate he called attention to the need of more rooms for the Sunday School and the congregation voted to remodel the building. During these changes religious services were transferred to the old church.

By adding a chapel to the west side of the church building and elevating the floor of the auditorium, space was made below for a modern heating plant with two ample furnaces. In this room there have been many merry-makings. In addition to the chapel, two large class rooms were obtained by this rearrangement. Electric lighting was available from the then new village light plant. The new chapel, which can be thrown open to the auditorium, was provided with chairs, the whole church redecorated and carpeted, making a most attractive church home. A piano had been presented in January, 1914, by a group of young women of the church and community.

The church was rededicated June 6, 1915. The Sunday School, meeting at 10 a.m., exceeded all former attendance records. Dr. Rothrock of Cleveland delivered the address at the church service and a number of Cincinnati Congregationalists were visitors. Minter C. Morris read a sketch of the church history and as church treasurer reported that the remodeling had cost $5,000, all of which except $300 had been paid.

At the evening service, the Rev. Seely K. Tompkins spoke. The building was crowded at both services as the members of the church showed their appreciation of the generosity which had made the rededication possible.

In this year (1915) also, the Rev. and Mrs. Spencer E. Evans, children of the church, presented a modern silver communion service to replace the silver tankard, which the mother church of Llanbrynmair sent by the Rev. B. W. Chidlaw in 1840 to the Paddy's Run church.

During the first World War the church was used continuously. W. R. Reeves, a recreational leader in Cincinnati, conducted neighborhood "sings" in a filled auditorium. During the winters of 1916-1917 and 1917-1918 A. W. Martin of Miami University conducted a community chorus of ninety members, presenting the results of their labors in a concert each spring. On the afternoon of November 11, 1918, a brief Thanksgiving service was held at the front entrance to the church lawn and a large flag raised on a flag-pole set for the purpose.

In 1931 a new organ for the church and a smaller one for the primary room were installed.

In August, 1933, the church celebrated its one hundred and thirtieth birthday with nearly a week of festivities, a home-coming picnic on Thursday, and an antique show throughout the days. On Saturday evening three historical papers were read and an address given by Dr. W. O. Thompson and on Sunday special music by the choir and the sermon by Dr. Thompson completed the anniversary celebration.

In 1943 a committee of women of the church was appointed to collaborate with the trustees on improvements. One organization in the church had accumulated $1,000 for such purposes. The regular church services were again transferred to the community house for the summer. Repairs and redecoration were completed by September and the Sunday School and church met on the first Sunday of the month in a building immaculate inside and out. The 140th anniversary was celebrated September 26 with the Rev. L. C. Talmage, former minister, as speaker.

The goal of the membership has always been "Keep the Church Open." This has been possible when the church has been without a pastor by drawing on Lane Seminary in Cincinnati and Miami University whose able professors have been willing to serve in need.

This somewhat detailed history of the "new" church, occupied since 1856, is to place on record the endeavors of the community to live up to the ideals of our pioneer ancestors in this valley.

From Welsh to English

The problem of the language of the homeland is one which has to be settled by any group which migrates. It is one which solves itself slowly when immigration stops by the processes of birth and death.

The first church organization in the Paddy's Run valley, that of the Whitewater Congregational Church, was English-speaking, but within a few years when the congregation at what is now Shandon became limited to the settlers in the immediate region, conditions were different.

The problem of shifting from the Welsh to the English language came as soon as the children were sent to school, which, according to Chidlaw, was in 1807. All the children of the Welsh pioneers learned the Welsh language, if for no other reason to prevent the old folks from having secrets. Each year the balance shifted toward the new language and each wave of immigration added strength to the Welsh contingent.

I had the privilege, one day, of hearing an old lady who had been too proud to learn to speak English, but not above learning to understand it, talk with my father who had forgotten how to speak Welsh, but still retained his childhood understanding of the language. I was exactly in the position you are when you hear some one telephoning. If it is simple enough, you can infer what the person at the other end of the line is saying.

The settlers from the older states knew no Welsh, so for many years there was an English service Sunday morning and a Welsh service in the afternoon. The double pastorate of Rees Lloyd and Thomas Thomas was set up in 1820 to meet this condition, but because of friction it lasted only three years. The Sunday School started in 1819 by Benjamin Lloyd, son of the Rev. Rees Lloyd, must have preceded or followed the

THE OLD GRAVEYARD AND THE CHURCHES

morning service and I am sure was conducted in English rather than Welsh.

By the time the second church building was occupied (1856), the number of those speaking Welsh was so reduced that they gathered as a Sunday School class and met in the old church. Except for two ministers, the Rev. John W. Browne and the Rev. Thomas Thomas, all the preachers up to the Rev. David Wilson (1861) spoke both languages. After the Civil War the problem had disappeared as far as church services were concerned, to appear again in the case of the German United Brethren Church years later.

Pastors of the Congregational Church, 1803-1944

John W. Browne, 1803-1812.
Rees Lloyd, 1817-1823.
Thomas Thomas, 1820-1827.
Thomas G. Roberts, 1828-1833.
Evan Roberts, several months, 1833-1834.
B. W. Chidlaw, 1836-1844.
Ellis Howell, 1844-1845.
J. H. Jones, 1845-1851.
James Pryse, 1855-1861.
D. W. Wilson, 1861-1863.
J. M. Thomas, 1863-1865.
H. R. Price, 1866-1870.
J. C. Thompson, 1870-1871.
George Candee, 1872-1875.
John L. Davies, 1876-1881.
D. F. Davies, 1884-1889.
Frank Foster, 1893-1897.
A. F. Bradley, 1897-1898.
C. A. Gleason, 1898-1901.
Morgan P. Jones, 1902-1908.
J. K. Higginbotham, 1908-1912.
S. D. Wellwood, 1913-1922.
Horace Hastings, 1925-1927.
L. Curtis Talmage, 1929-1938.
M. G. Jones, 1938-1942.
J. M. Peyton, 1944————.

Local Doctors

Dr. William Thomas I, 1825-1831, son-in-law of William Gwilym. (Followed by one of his students, Dr. Silas Roll, for a year or more. Dr. Blackford succeeded Dr. Roll and died in 1839.)

Dr. William Thomas II, 1837-1852. (His wife was the aunt of Mrs. H. H. Robinson, Sr.)
Dr. N. R. Morris, 1851-1853.
Dr. Griffin McKendree Shaw, 1854-1863.
Dr. Joseph Roberts, 1851-1866.
Dr. Peter Brooks, 1872————.
Dr. Samuel J. M. Marshall, 1876.
Dr. Armstrong.
Dr. S. K. Hamer.
Dr. H. Williamson, 1879-1882 (?).
Dr. John Masters, ————1892.
Dr. ———— Thomin, 1893-1896 (?).
Dr. Cary T. Hull.
Dr. Burkert Clark, 1913-1939.

CHAPTER XVI

THE SCHOOLHOUSES OF PADDY'S RUN

ACCORDING to Chidlaw (Appendix III) the first school was that of Miss Polly Wiley in 1807. It was located south of the village and somewhere west of the present pike, on land which John Vaughan had sold to James Nicholas in 1803, now occupied by Harry Evans.

In 1810 a schoolhouse (see Appendix III) was built by the community. There is no mention of its location. Since the grist mill was at Morgantown over on the Dry Fork and all bridle paths led in that direction it might have been on the hill southwest of the future village.

When Ohio's primary school system was organized in 1826, the center of the district was on the hill close to the road from Hamilton through Paddy's Run to New Haven and Harrison, and there the schoolhouse was built. A log house with one room, it was used for twenty-five years. William Bebb was the first teacher, his certificate to teach having been signed by James Shields.

After it was no longer used as a school, the house was moved into the village close to Hugh Williams' blacksmith shop, and having been weatherboarded it can be recognized as a log house only when the termites swarm.

For the fourth school building land was purchased, April 10, 1852, from George Milholland nearer the New Haven road and a two-room weatherboarded building was put up. Both the third and fourth school houses were near the center of District No. 7 and out of the village. The school board in 1852 was William Atherton, Thomas Appleton and David Atherton.

Authorized by the legislative act for the organization of Special School Districts, the New London Special School District was established December 10, 1869, and the first board members were Jacob Scheel, Evan Evans and Thomas Appleton. In 1871 three acres were purchased in the village and the four-room brick schoolhouse still existing was constructed under the direction of Griffith Morris, Abner Francis, and Evan Evans, then composing the board.

This building, and others rented, served as the high school grew larger until, after sixty-six years, the New London Special District was included in 1937 in the present Ross Township High School area.

The old schoolyard and house are at present held by the trustees of the Congregational Church. The library for the community is now located in the north room of the first floor of the building.

Teachers—Academy and Special School District

1858-	D. W. McClung, Hugh W. Scott.
1863-	Mark Williams, D. W. Wilson.
1865-	James A. Clark.
1870-	Samuel McClelland.
1871-	Florence Shafer.
1872-1880	James A. Clark.
1880-1883	J. T. Trisler.
1883-1886	J. P. Sharkey.
1886-1889	James Keeling.
1889-1890	Elmer Schultze.
1890-1893	H. B. Smith.
1893-1895	James Bickley.
1895-1896	F. DuBois.
1896-1898	R. A. Jameson.
1898-1905	J. A. Goshorn.
1905-1906	David C. Jones.
1906-1909	R. Burton Reed.
1909-1930	Stanley Rowland.
1931-1937	J. H. Kilburn.

The following were teachers in the grade school of the New London Special District. The list was compiled from memory by Alice Scott Robinson (Mrs. Henry H. Robinson), who does not claim it to be complete:

Jane Atherton Scott (in the old church, 1870-1871).
India L. Davis Whipple.
Abbie Appleton Gwaltney.

Sallie Salsbery.
Anne Peate.
Mattie D. Jones.
Fannie Maxwell.
Katie Scheel.
Jessie Brown Scheel.
Allie Lowe Gillespie.
Patty Karr Dowling.
Alma Joyce Scott.
Sallie Jones Davies.
Mary Jonte Shearer.

CHAPTER XVII

THE LIBRARIES OF PADDY'S RUN
by Martha Francis and S. R. Williams

THE FIRST State Commissioner of Common Schools of Ohio called attention to a library founded in a community in the state by the contributions of its pioneer settlers. "To the inspirations from this library," to quote the commissioner, "some of the finest names in our annals owe the impulse to a distinguished career."

The history of this library and its successors follows: At the opening of the country west of the Great Miami for settlement, the community of Paddy's Run, or Shandon as it is now (twenty miles northwest of Cincinnati), was established in large part by a group of emigrants from Wales seeking to better themselves financially, intellectually and spiritually. The most of the incoming settlers from Virginia and the Carolinas were of the same type, and one of the first deeds of the infant community was the founding of a church, a Congregational church which celebrated its centennial in 1903.

The next move was the beginning of a private school. William Bebb, one of the pupils of this first school, established one of his own, the Bebb boarding school, which did its share toward educating boys from the near-by town of Cincinnati.

The third step was the starting of a library.

In the old library record book the first dates of withdrawal are in the year 1817. There are many entries in 1818. The library so flourished that on February 1, 1821, we find an agreement of the Union Library Company of Morgan and Crosby Townships which contains eighteen articles and is signed by the following: John Halstead, Brant Agnew, Hartman Dantreece, William McCune, David Owens, James H. Waer, Edward Bebb, James McCune, John Cleaver, Joseph Yaeger, David Hornick, Moses Nutt, Alex Rittenhouse, George

Yaeger, Joseph Brown, Hugh Smith, David Agnew, Henry Sefton, Peter Pulse, Ephraim Carmack, Jeremiah Buffington, Abel Appleton, Robert Mahaffey, John Vaughan, James Shields.

This document is endorsed further as follows:

STATE OF OHIO, SEVENTH CIRCUIT

I, Joshua Collett, President Judge of the Court of Common Pleas for said seventh circuit, approve the within Articles of Association.
August 29, 1821. (Signed) Joshua Collett.

We have examined and do approve of the within Articles of Association.
April 2, 1821. (Signed) V. Burnett, John McLean,
Judges Supreme Court, Ohio.

Received and recorded, May 18th, 1822, in Book II, pages 137 and 138 by C. K. Smith, Recorder of Butler County, Ohio. Fees, $1.12½.

Shares in this Library Association cost $3 each and 65 were taken. One can hardly realize now what an influence $200 worth of books would have on a community which had no newspapers and few privately owned books except the Bible.

From the record of withdrawals of books, since there is no catalogue of the library extant, we find that it included the following books: Plutarch's Lives; Pictorial Cincinnati, a two-volume work; Lives of the Poets, Riley's Narratives, Brooks Gazetteer, Lewis and Clark's Expedition, Aesop's Fables, Davis' Agriculture, Park's Travels, Gay's Fables, Chaptol's Chemistry, Life of Bonaparte, Essay on Sheep, Brydone's (also written Drybones) Tours, Guthrie's Geography, Ramsay's United States, Clark on Slavery, Blair's Lectures, and the Spirit of Despotism.

These books were drawn in turn by the subscribers and many were renewed or redrawn many times.

The withdrawal page of Edward Bebb, father of the future Governor Bebb, was as follows: 1817, 9; 1818, 12; 1819, 11; 1820, 15; 1821, 10; 1822, 12; 1823, 14; 1824, 7; 1825, 4.

William D. Jones, store-keeper, was not such a bookworm. His record is rather light: 1818, 4; 1819, 2; 1820, 3; 1821, 2; 1822, 0; 1823, 0; 1824, 2.

Moreover, he was fined a bit (12½ cents) for two folded leaves on a returned book and thirteen bits ($1.62½) for keeping out Brook's Gazetteer for thirteen weeks, so possibly ambition was quenched untimely in his case.

The Association library was kept at the mill where everybody's grist was ground. This mill was in an extremely rough country in order to avoid digging a long race and the roads to it were mere bridle paths, passable for a horse and rider with his sack of grain. In later years when supplies could be obtained in larger quantities on the improved turnpikes from Cincinnati and Hamilton, the mill fell into disuse and the library was lost. At present, one of the two volumes of Lives of the Poets is still available.

In 1852 a second library association was formed, probably on the suggestion of Evan R. Bebb of New York City, son of the pioneer Edward Bebb and brother of the governor. This was restricted to the one neighborhood, and thirty-one shares of $5 each were paid in. Mr. Bebb donated $10, gave from the best of his private library and interested his business partner, Edward C. Graham, so that Mr. Graham sent to the library a number of valuable books on travel, history and science. Mr. Bebb interested himself also in helping select the books and place the orders. At that time in paying the book bill the exchange on New York cost one half of one per cent.

Other contributors to this library were Tom Corwin, Robert C. Schenck and Lewis D. Campbell of the House of Representatives and U. S. Senator George E. Pugh. This library was housed in the Atherton home west of the village. At first shareholders only were permitted to use the library. Later, on payment of 50 cents yearly, others were admitted to the privileges and when a written order from a member permitted the withdrawal of books, it became virtually a free library.

When the schoolhouse was built in New London Special District, a room was built for books donated by the shareholders to the community and administered by the teachers.

In 1885 books given by the state as the Ohio School Library, and forgotten for years in the attic of a former school director, were repossessed by J. P. Sharkey, then the superintendent of schools. His report to the Ohio school commissioner for 1885 explains how, by a mid-winter oyster supper and a summer picnic, $100 a year was obtained for necessary repairs and a few new books.

In this way the library served the teachers and students in the school and the townspeople interested for the next thirty years, but feeling the need of more books, in 1915 a circular letter was sent to high school alumni, former students and friends, soliciting books for the community library. This brought a generous response in gifts of worth-while books and in money to purchase others. About 350 volumes were added at this time, thus bringing the available books to 1,500, an unusual number for so small a community. The library was recatalogued at that time.

Records show that the library was open for withdrawal of books Saturday afternoons during the summer months of 1917. The graduating classes showed their interest by gifts. The class of 1909 purchased a reading table to be used in the library and later classes set aside money to be used in the purchase of books.

In 1920 when Dr. Mark Williams, well known missionary to China and a former Paddy's Run boy, died, he left $200 as an endowment fund for the library. This money was invested and the interest was used in book purchases. In later years additional gifts have been added to this fund by individual persons, by the high school class of 1924 and a sum transferred from a community lecture fund, the amount at the present time being $420.

In 1931 the Shandon Library Association was reorganized and has remained active. The payment of dues entitles the members to the right to vote on the policies of the association.

With the organization and combining of the present Ross School District, the library was moved into a room on the second floor of the science building. Prof. E. W. King and others of the Miami University staff assisted local people in recataloguing and repairing the books. A few books, seldom if ever read, were taken from the shelves. An exchange of a number of duplicate books was made with Miami. Shandon was fortunate in thus acquiring some valuable books of reference.

The commercial department of the school took charge of the catalogue files and the manual training classes made shelves and book ends. A student librarian was in the library room during each school period; so that five days each week the library was available to the public as well as to the students. Mr. Kilburn, superintendent of the school, was intensely interested and anxious that all pupils and those living in the community benefit from the library.

When the present Ross High School building was occupied, this library remained in Shandon. When the old school property was sold at public auction in the spring of 1940, the high school building and grounds were bought by the trustees of the Congregational Church with funds subscribed by the people of the community and by former loyal Shandon residents, among whom Dr. Albert Shaw was a generous donor.

The books were transfered to the northwest room on the first floor. This was a real moving day. By the cooperation of many workers the shelves were set in place in their new location the same afternoon that the books were removed from them and very soon thereafter the books were on the shelves ready for circulation.

For the last several years a ways and means committee has sponsored successful scrap-iron and waste paper drives twice each year. The whole-hearted response on the part of people in the neighborhood has brought in worth-while sums to the library treasury. The book committee, appointed each year, purchases current books and necessary replacements. The past year children's books were stressed. Some choice books have been given as memorials and a number of excellent books are received by the library each year.

The library is open for the withdrawal of books one afternoon each week with a few exceptions durings bitter weather. The gift of an oil-burner has made the room usable in winter. At present the library is open each Sunday afternoon.

On November 14, 1943, an open house was held at which a speaker gave an interesting talk related to books and libraries to an appreciative audience. Also at the Christmas season that year a story hour for children was a feature.

In 1944 Mrs. Elizabeth Thomas Owens Schultz, great-granddaughter of William Gwilym, on whose farm most of the village of Shandon is located, sent sixty or more desirable books to the library, showing her interest in this worth-while activity of the community.

This is a project that always requires something more. It is never complete. The functioning of a library is possible only through the cooperation of many loyal, interested people of the community. The officers of the Library Association, the present ones as well as those who have served in previous years, have given unselfishly of their time. With this interest the library will continue to be a vital part in the life of the Shandon community.

The Daniel Wilkins house, 1845-47. The Roberts octagonal house, 1858, as added to the John Halstead guest house, 1825. The Abner Francis house, 1857. The birthplace of Albert Shaw, built 1842. The John Vaughan house, built 1814-16.

The Col. Griffin Halstead house, 1828. The John Evans house, 1842. The James Shields house, 1819-1913. The (Butterfield) Morris house.

CHAPTER XVIII

HOUSES

The John Vaughan House

MARTHA EVANS ADAMS suggests that certain stones in the "cherry tree" field, east of Paddy's Run and near the center of the Vaughan half section, may be the remains of the foundation of the Vaughan log house. The second house, built in 1816, was the first brick house in the neighborhood and both it and the frame barn, built about the same time, were often used for church services before the erection of the old meeting house ten years later. The house is on the first gravel knoll east of the village and the bricks for it were burned on the place. The owner's initials, J. ("I" with a center cross-bar the letter means "J") V. appear in black bricks below the east gable. It is a saddle-bag house with unequal extensions back. The front door faces south and is set not quite in the middle. As a result one coming down the front stairs is not directly in line with the open front door.

The spacious front hall is wainscoted in walnut both above and below stairs and through the wide doors to the left and to the right you can see the man-sized fireplaces used in that day of unlimited wood for protection against winter's cold. Each one of these, on the first floor at least, had a crane and hooks for pots and kettles.

North of the large rooms narrower rooms extended back on either side leaving in the middle a partially roofed-over back porch where the duties of the household were carried on except in cold weather.

The large rooms upstairs, similar to those below, differed only that to the east, on one side of the fireplace an angular staircase made its parsimonious way to the unfinished attic above, while elsewhere large cupboards flanked the fireplaces both above and below.

The light in the attic was derived from two small windows, one at each end of the house in the gable. This light was adequate only on bright days in the early morning and near sunset when the light pointed directly at the windows.

This first brick house set a high standard for the community and most of those which followed were built on the saddle-bag plan with a central hall and four large rooms, two below and two above. Smaller rooms with lower ceilings could be either two additions with porch between as in this case, or one back on one side or the other, or one in the middle continuing back of the hall. The high ceilings of the front rooms made them more comfortable through the warm part of the year and hard to heat in the winter.

As far as I know, all these brick walls were solidly built, without a central air space and therefore these houses are not as warm as the weatherboarded, wooden houses which followed them. They are, however, more nearly fire-proof.

When, after a hundred years of weathering, a Vaughan window sill needed replacing, it was found that instead of being built up of several pieces as ours now are, the sill proper with its outward slant, the stool behind the sash, and the apron below the stool were all hewed out of a single slab of black walnut and the upper members of the window frame mortised into it. I am afraid to say how many inches wide the window ledge is behind the sash, but it makes a fine place for potted plants, or for a couple of small children to play "outside" the heavy curtains and concealed from the occupants of the room.

I am told that a modern repair man, instead of duplicating the worn ledge, cut the Gordian knot by chiseling out the outer damaged portion and setting a slab of cement in its place.

William, the son of John and Martha Vaughan, was born in the log house. John Vaughan's second wife was Ruth Crosby, whose funeral was the first service in the old church, completed in August, 1825. His third marriage was to Mrs. Mary Brightwell and later he is reported to have said tactfully that he first married a Welshwoman, then a New Englander, and then one of German descent and he thought he had done better each time.

William Vaughan married Mary Bebb, daughter of Edward and Margaret Bebb, in 1824. Their children were John Green, 1827; Martha Ann, 1832; William Crosby, 1834; and Mary Bebb, 1846.

William Vaughan was the first postmaster of Paddy's Run and the postoffice was in their brick house from 1831 to 1847.

John G. Vaughan's wife, Ann Davies, died April 30, 1856, and he moved to Illinois before the Civil War. Martha Ann married Abner Francis in 1856 and Mrs. Vaughan with her remaining son and daughter kept on with the farm. When Mary Vaughan married Rees Evans they lived with Mrs. Vaughan and here their children, Hannah, Martha, Ed, and Will were born.

The Shields House, 1819-1912
by Clara Francis

Mr. and Mrs. Shields were married in Virginia, came to Paddy's Run in 1804, and settled on the east half of section 36 in what a few years later was to be Morgan Township. The location of their cabin is not known. Soon after it was built Mrs. Shields left her infant daughter Maria in charge of a nurse girl and went on an exploring expedition. She must have missed some turning and became lost. After considerable walking she discovered a log house and knocked at the door. When it was opened she saw her baby in the arms of the nurse.

A good many of the twelve Shields children must have been born in this log house, as the brick house was built in 1819. This date is arrived at in the following way. Betsy Reese, oldest daughter of Squire John C. Jones, was born the year this house was built. In 1912 Mark Williams preached at Shandon and wrote his family that he had had a pleasant visit with Robert Reese and his wife, both of them 93 years of age.

The bricks for the house were burned on the low ground in front of the site. These bricks were not uniform in size so when the house was taken down in 1912 the salable bricks could be used only for flue linings and similar rough work. The boys must have had a hand in the brick molding because bricks were found marked James and Jane and Shields. This last one was presented to Mrs. Parthena Wilkins Jones, a grandchild, and she set great store by it.

The house had a beautiful setting on a terrace on the east slope of a hill which is one of the few remains of the eastern wall of the old Dry Fork valley. The present Paddy's Run has had to bend in a large half circle into the eastern part of its valley because of this elevation. Beyond it straightens into the old Dry Fork path again.

The house was L-shaped, about fifty feet across the front and forty-five, more or less, in depth to the west. In front there were two rooms, 16 by 18 feet, separated by a wide hall whose back door opened onto a large porch. There was also a window to the west on the stair landing. In summer with both doors and the window open the hall was most pleasant as there was always a cool breeze there.

The south room had two windows on the east and two on the west wall looking out onto the long open porch. On the south wall there was a fireplace with a high Colonial wood mantel flanked by shelved cupboards, each with a half door above and below. This room had but one door, the one from the hall.

One entered the living room at the north by a doorway near the foot of the stairs. This room had three windows, two on the east side and one on the north instead of a cupboard as in the south room. The fireplace and mantel and northeast cupboard were like those in the other room. All the floors in the house were of wide oak boards.

The enormous kitchen was directly west of this room. In the middle of its west wall was a large brick fireplace with a heavy iron crane provided with a number of pothooks. There was a large fire-board to cover the fireplace when it was not in use. There were cupboards with shelves on each side of the fireplace as in the other rooms. The north and south walls of this kitchen each had a door and a window. There was a half story attic room over the kitchen reached by a winding box staircase on the southeast wall. The only windows in this attic were on either side of the kitchen chimney.

The south kitchen door opened on the southwest porch, which was L-shaped with an open railing around the west and south sides. There was a pantry on the west side just next to the kitchen. A door in the porch floor led down a wooden stair to the basement under the front part of the house. It had a dirt floor and was lighted by two narrow windows in the foundation. A large wooden meat block was used to set things on.

Beginning again at the front hall, the stairs started by the living room door, went up to a landing on which one turned and ascended two more steps to the level of the second floor. The banister was small and the spindles delicate and continued around the stair well to the north wall of the hall.

The south bedroom, with two front windows and a window in the middle of the west wall, was to the right. On the south wall there were two closets, a fireplace, and a high door to the attic over the main house. The attic stairs started two steps out in the room and twisted after one went through the door. The clothes closet under these attic stairs is remembered as always full of white and colored starched gingham dresses.

To the left of the door by which one entered this bedroom was a narrow door leading into a room over the front hall. It had one front window. A heavy molding around part of the wall about two feet below the ceiling was fitted with many heavy wooden pegs for hanging clothes.

The north bedroom had three windows, a fireplace, and a closet matching those of the living room below. This closet was provided with a shelf above the hanging space and a floor raised to about the level of the base-board. It was much easier to hang or take down clothing from the pegs when you were small if you stepped on this raised floor.

Considering that there were twelve Shields children, it seems that the provision for hanging clothes was not excessive. They are as follows (but I do not vouch for the order of birth):

Maria (m. Jenkins).
David D.
Matthew Russell.
Joseph W. (Wilson).
Martha Ann (m. Kumler).
Samuel D.
Jane (m. Isaac McClelland).

James Madison.
Eliza D. (m. Daniel Wilkins).
Sarah P. (m. King).
Thomas J.
John Wright.

After the Shields, the family of Jonathan Butterfield occupied this house and when David Francis and Etta Jones were married in 1888 (February), they began housekeeping here. The chief change David Francis made was in the entrance to the place. The Shields and Butterfields entered through a gate on the township road by a short lane to the barnyard. The new entrance was at the start of the hill toward Shandon and directly into the house yard, passing a triangular garden along the north section line. All their children were born here.

Ethel, b. December 27, 1888—d. February 12, 1936.
Howard, b. January 11, 1890—d. September 27, 1893.
Alice, b. June 22, 1891.
Abner, b. November 13, 1894 (m. Gladys Guthrie).
Clara, b. November 6, 1896—d. January 8, 1945.
Florence, b. May 4, 1898.
Martha, b. December 11, 1901.
Roland D., b. June 30, 1903 (m. Ada Schradin).

As time went on the outer walls seemed to demand major repairs, so the old brick house was taken down and replaced by a weather-boarded frame building on the same site. This was completed in January, 1913.

The Halstead Houses

(Taken from "Paddy's Run Papers" by Murat Halstead. Written in 1894)

"In 1805 when John Halstead left his flooded Miami River bottom farm for the valley of the Paddy's Run he bought the north half of section 30 from Maurice Jones. By a spring at the slope of the hills where he had stopped his wagon under a mulberry tree, he built a temporary house of rails, filling in the cracks with sod, moss, and wet clay.

"In 1806 he built a large, two-story house of hewn slippery elm logs with puncheon floors of ash. The trees selected for puncheons had to be of even growth so as to split straight. They were halved, the flat sides planed smooth, the sides hewn to a close joint and each tree thus made two planks. The sides with the bark were down, of course, and the floors were as solid as marble.

"There were two long strings of out-buildings; stables, corn cribs, a smoke house, a milk house, pens for pigs and a shelter for cows, a wagon shed or two and a log barn, altogether quite a village."

(Told by Alice Scott Robinson, 1943)

"In 1825 great-grandfather built a frame house, mostly of walnut, in the yard where the log house stood. This was his guest house and in this house his son Griffin lived when he married, until he and his bride moved to the house by the northern spring where Murat Halstead was born. The guest house consisted of a cellar, one room on the first floor and a second-story room. A walnut cupboard and a cherry cupboard, one of them a corner cupboard and the other rectangular, were both built by great-grandfather and are in good condition.

"To the north side of this guest house an octagonal building was added in 1858-1859 by Dr. Joseph Roberts, who married my great-aunt Sarah, daughter of John Halstead. This was planned by a Cincinnati architect, Plimpton by name. Much of the woodwork is walnut, the floors hardwood and the windows fitted with inside shutters.

"The plan of rooms seemed very convenient. The front door leads into a hall which has doors into a west and an east room. The east room leads to the kitchen, once the first floor room of the guest house.

"The front stairs of cherry and walnut are considered unusually fine. Three clothes closets, two being three-cornered, in the hall were a great help to a big family. There was also a three-cornered hall bedroom above the front door which all youngsters loved. There were three square bedrooms upstairs and a bathroom. Its first tub was wooden and very long, the first 'set' bathtub in the neighborhood. (Anna B. Jones used to come over and enjoy it with me. I lived in the octagon house for sixty years and love every inch of it.)

(This house was occupied after 1872 by John M. Scott and Helen Halstead Scott and their children, by Henry Robinson,

Sr., and Alice Scott Robinson, and now by Mr. and Mrs. Henry Halstead Robinson and daughter Virginia.)

(This octagon house is thought to have been the inspiration for the house which former Governor William Bebb built in Kalorama Park, District of Columbia, when he was on the staff of the U. S. Patent Office in Washington. Mr. Bebb frequently visited his sister, Mary Bebb Vaughan, in Paddy's Run. The house built by Bebb is still standing in Kalorama Park.)

"In the yard, thirty feet from John Halstead's log house and fifty feet from the guest house, a two-room brick house was built about 1832 for a kitchen and dining room for great-grandfather who, Southern style, did not care for cooking to be done in his main house. Dr. Roberts used it for his offices. Uncle Murat's initials still show on the mortar between the bricks.

'Griffin Halstead's house in the sycamore grove was built in 1828. It is a frame house of 'bank' style built into the hillside. On the lower floor, the kitchen faces south, the north wall is mostly below ground, and the side walls partly so. With the idea of warmth these walls were about eighteen inches thick. The stairway up was quaint and twisted, with a landing near the kitchen fireplace.

"The living room, with front door to the north, had a few steps down to the level of the ground. A walnut partition divided this living room from a bedroom.

"The most charming and lovable place was an upstairs in-porch facing south from the living room and bounded on the east and west by bedrooms. The view from here was wonderful; one could see the greater part of the valley. Mother said that from this porch she could easily hear Mr. Chidlaw preaching in the sugar maple grove where the Griffith Morris house now stands."

The Robinson Log House

No one knows who built the well-preserved hewed-log house on lot 22 in the village of Shandon. Tradition, embalmed in a newspaper article by Clark B. Firestone, gives the date as 1803, but tradition has no place in history except as a backing for something more trustworthy. Anyhow the date, 1803, is early for so elaborate a two-story building made from hewn logs. The dimensions, 30 by 22 feet, are large for a first cabin. They involve cutting enough straight, slim logs 32 feet long for two sides of the building within easy dragging distance of the site. Whereas if the house had been built for the first occupant we are sure of, the Rev. Thomas Thomas in 1820, there were roads and heavy wagons and teams to bring selected logs from any distance. Since by 1820 there were many inhabitants in the village, some hospitable neighbor would have given the Thomas family shelter while the logs were being hewn for such an aristocratic residence.

The interior would suggest that the house had been prepared with school rooms in mind. Both Mr. and Mrs. Thomas taught from 1820 to 1827. He had high school pupils from as far away as Dayton and Mrs. Thomas trained the local girls in plain and ornamental sewing. Samplers of wondrous stitchings were produced by Mrs. Thomas' pupils and since she exemplified the faraway London, England, from which she came, the village where she held forth has had New London as one of its many names.

There is one first floor room 22 by 15 feet, and another narrower by the width of the hall. An enclosed stairway leads up from between the rooms and the wood partitions are fastened with screws rather than nails, so that it might not have been too difficult to shift their locations. The unusual number of windows also suggests school rooms. The early cabin had not more than one window, if that, covered with a sheet of oiled paper. I would contend that the building itself says that it was not built in 1803 but later.

In 1827 Mr. Thomas was called to preach in Venice and history again fails us. The first resident physician, Dr. William Thomas No. 1 died in 1831 and his namesake, though unrelated, Dr. William Thomas No. 2, must have bought this property after 1834 because in the rather detailed history of the deadly local epidemic of Asiatic cholera in July of that year there is no mention of a doctor of that name.

Dr. Thomas the second was a graduate of the University of Bristol and had been for a time with the Whitewater Shakers, where his work was gardening, so though his vocation was medicine his avocation was horticulture and a very elaborate planting plan has survived in the log house, showing the trees and plants he hoped to develop in his grounds. His office and stables were north of the house and the width of the lot away. The private entrance to the stable later had buildings on its north side and was known as Bevan's Lane.

The main interest at this point is that it was this Dr. Thomas who settled the location of the large hotel and store-building which H. H. Robinson built on the Cincinnati-Brookville pike about 1850.

To explain this fully it is best to start with Samuel Robinson back in New Jersey. He married Mariah Ent, daughter of Major (War of 1812) Charles Ent and Mary Johnson Ent. Their son, Henry Hidlay Robinson, was born May 16, 1816, and when he was two years old the Robinsons left New Jersey for Ohio, probably because Mrs. Robinson's father, Major Ent, was moving into the new country.

At a later date Joseph Glancy and his wife, Hettie Rittenhouse Glancy, went to Morristown, Indiana, where on July 10, 1828, their daughter Josephine was born. Some years later Mrs. Glancy died and Joseph Glancy came to Paddy's Run to his sister-in-law, the wife of Dr. William Thomas No. 2, and left with them his motherless daughter Josephine. For a number of years she made her home with her uncle and aunt and attended the district school on the hill.

As time went on Mr. Glancy started a hotel in Keithsburg, Illinois, on the Mississippi River just opposite where the Iowa River enters. It occurred to him that his daughter was a fairly well-grown girl and would be useful in his business, so he went to Paddy's Run and took Josephine back with him to Keithsburg. This was perfectly legal since in those days the labor of minor children was an asset, but Josephine did not approve. She did not want to stop her schooling or to work the long hours necessary in a house of public entertainment.

She was an observing girl and one day recognized Giles Richards of Colerain village on the Miami when he was in Keithsburg on a business trip, selling the products of the

Colerain woolen mills. Finding a chance to speak with him privately, she told him how homesick she was for her aunt and friends in Paddy's Run. He said that, of course, there was nothing he could do about it, but that the steamboat was leaving down river at midnight and if she were on it he might be able to help her. So she waited on the table that evening and washed the dishes as usual and as a final gesture scrubbed the dining room floor. Slipping on board the boat a few minutes before it was due to leave, she hid for the night. The next morning when Mr. Richards knew she was on board, he spoke to the passengers, telling the facts about the homesick girl and they chipped in with money enough to buy her a steamboat ticket to Cincinnati. I think Mr. Richards delivered her to her aunt in the log house on Lot 22. At any rate her father never came after her, she was able to attend school again and on December 7, 1847, she married Henry Robinson.

Hugh Williams had built a substantial brick house in the angle between the Millville road and the Brookville pike. In 1848 the Robinsons leased this house for use as a hotel with the privilege of purchase at a stated price. Doctor Thomas convinced them that with more space they could build a better hotel and store building on the end of his lot facing the Brookville pike at the north end of the village. This they did about 1850 and the three-story building is nearing its centennial. Many traveling between Cincinnati and Brookville by bus or private conveyance spent the night in this hotel, which also housed a general store and was often the local postoffice.

The first Robinson child born in the new home was Erastus.

The following children were born to the Robinsons:

William Walter, November 11, 1848.
Mary Mae, December 17, 1849.
Cornelia, July 9, 1851.
Erastus, February 26, 1853.
Susan, July 16, 1854.
Alexander Rittenhouse, July 9, 1856 (m. Ellen Williamson).
Hettie Maria, March 22, 1858.
Samuel Glancy, October 11, 1859 (m. Lizzie Duckwall).
Amy, February 26, 1861.
Evaline Celia, September 17, 1862.
Charles E., May 12, 1864.

Henry H., Jr., November 12, 1865 (m. Alice Scott).
Josephine, May 27, 1868 (m. Warner Scott).
Anne Amelia, July 11, 1870.

Erastus studied medicine with Dr. Peter Brooks, who practiced in Paddy's Run in the early 1870's. He was graduated from the Miami Medical College with the degree M.D. in 1876. He married Emma Evans soon thereafter and practiced in Trenton, Butler County. His wife died within the year. In 1881 he married Mrs. Mary Jane (Williams) Cochran and moved to Osgood, Indiana, where their son, Clinton Kirby, was born January 1, 1883; died August 12, 1914. They returned to Paddy's Run early in 1885 and made their home in the Thomas log house, where Paul R. was born April 22, 1885. Both their sons graduated from Miami, Kirby in 1904 and Paul in 1907.

The John Evans House
by Mrs. Fred Walther and Mrs. Ruth Wilson

John Evans was born in the parish of Llanbrynmair, Montgomeryshire, North Wales, July 17, 1795, the son of Evan and Elizabeth Evans. He came to America on the ship Clio and after a voyage of eighty-two days, landed at Baltimore, Maryland, on September 8, 1818. From Baltimore he journeyed to Paddy's Run, Ohio. He stayed with his uncle, John Vaughan, Sr., until he decided what he should undertake.

On February 16, 1821, he was married to Sarah Nicholas, the second daughter of James and Mary Nicholas, born on Paddy's Run March 16, 1806. Fourteen children were born to them. Their names, dates of birth, and the people they married, are as follows:

Mary, December 9, 1821 (m. Maurice F. Jones).
Evan J., November 4, 1823 (m., 1st, ―― Richards; 2nd, Susan, her sister).
Eliza, March 26, 1825 (m. David D. Davies).
William, July 7, 1827 (m. Jane Thomas).
James, February 26, 1829 (no record).
Ann, November 26, 1830 (m. Edward Jones).
Martha, August 17, 1832 (m. Robert Griffith).
John N., July 18, 1834 (m. Ann Elizabeth Watkins).
Robert, March 8, 1836 (m. Margaret Davies).

David, July 18, 1838; d. January 29, 1843.
Sarah, November 8, 1840 (m. Owen W. Davies).
Richard, December 1, 1842 (m. Marietta White).
Edward, August 24, 1845 (m. Mary Malvina Newsom).
George, January 19, 1850 (m. Orris White).

Sarah and John Evans began their married life in a log cabin which was located across the road some distance from the house of Miss Eliza Francis. A clump of locust trees marks the building site.

In 1842 they built the brick house, now owned by Mr. and Mrs. Ray Scott. It was built close to the newly established pike, somewhat over a mile east of Shandon towards Venice. The gate in the middle of the iron fence extending across the front yard has the name John Evans printed in the iron at the top.

The large porch, which covers the front door and the four first floor windows, has a continuous step across the front and at each end. A smaller side porch of the same style is at the right of the house.

The front door has two wooden panels at the bottom and at the top there are two red glass panels with white flowers and vines etched on them. A sill of stone lies in the doorway between the porch floor and the floor of the hall.

The ceilings throughout the house are nine feet high and the window sills in all the windows are eight inches wide. There is a fireplace in each room with mantels fifty-two inches across. The center of attraction of the parlor mantel was a Seth Thomas clock, now in the home of a grandson, Roger Evans. The doors leading from the hall, both upstairs and down, have unusual small brass knobs.

The meal-room or pantry was an exciting room. A grandson tells the story of seven cakes being placed in the meal-room by the hired girl for safe-keeping. Several of the third generation were visiting that day and were certain they would get caught if they stepped on the porch to get in the meal-room door. They could raise the window from the outside, but not high enough to crawl through. So one boy went to the barn and got a pitchfork to push through the window space, and by skillful manipulation there were only six cakes left for the family.

The wash-house, or summer kitchen, at the rear of the back porch was used more for cooking than the kitchen-dining room in the main part of the house. The dinner bell was in a belfry at the top of the summer kitchen to make it handy to ring for the men. The smoke house was at the end of this room and the cistern was in the floor of this kitchen. The floor around the cistern pump was partly flag-stones and partly brick. A work table, over seven feet long, three and a half feet wide and two feet and four inches high was used in this kitchen and is now in the possession of a great-granddaughter, Clara Francis. This same family has the copper kettle two feet across and fifteen inches high which would hold more than a bushel of apples in the process of making apple-butter.

The hall is eight feet wide, with oak floors whose boards run in groups, $9\frac{1}{2}$ inches, 7 inches, and 5 inches, then $9\frac{1}{2}$ and repeat the series. Each stair step is $10\frac{1}{2}$ by 39 inches. A plain rail of cherry and a number of small square spindles are held in place by six posts $3\frac{1}{2}$ inches square. The wall under the stairs on the first floor is made of wooden panels and a cupboard directly under the stairs is at the right of the paneled wall.

The upstairs rooms are similar to those below. Each room has four large hooks with wires extending from the ceiling. No one knows the purpose of these hooks. Some say that they held shelves for drying food and others that they supported quilting frames.

There is no entrance to the cellar from inside of the house. It is directly under the two rooms on the right of the house and deep stone steps lead down to it from the back. Each cellar window is protected by iron rods set in cement.

John Evans was a farmer and hog feeder. He both raised and bought hogs to fatten and sell, thereby acquiring the name of "Hog Johnnie," the name John Evans not being specific in a Welsh community. His son Richard often told how he, when five years old, drove the spring wagon home from Rushville, Indiana. His father had gone that far to buy hogs which were to be driven home to Paddy's Run. When a hog gave out it was loaded into the spring wagon to rest.

John Evans fed his hogs from a corncrib not far from his house which had a projection in front, roofed over. David Owens from Wales called it "Ould John Ivins' pilpit where he preach to the hogs."

The monument with watering troughs, which he erected on the hill between his home and the village in 1887, is a landmark in the community. The monument bears the inscription, "And now abideth Faith, Hope and Charity, these three, but the greatest of these is Charity. 1st Corinthians." His son Robert helped prepare the foundations and install the monument, brought out from Hamilton on a log-wagon drawn by five mules, two at the tongue and three abreast in the lead.

The monument in the cemetery at Shandon which marks the last resting place of Sarah and John Evans is of interest. It is Scotch granite and came as ballast on a ship from Scotland to this country. On it one reads that Sarah Evans died April 8, 1870, and John Evans on February 1, 1890.

The brick house which is the birthplace of Albert Shaw stands in the angle between the Millville road and the Brookville pike. It was built by Deacon Hugh Williams in 1843 and appears in the history of the Robinson family between 1847 and 1850.

In 1854 Dr. Griffin McKendree Shaw, who had been brought up in the Paddy's Run community and had practised medicine in Noblesville, Indiana, brought his family back to Paddy's Run to avoid the malaria in Noblesville.

He purchased the brick house and built an office adjoining it. He later bought all the remainder of the triangle up to the lane below the new church grounds.

He was a draft board official for Morgan Township in the Civil War until his sudden death from appendicitis in 1863. The family remained in the village for about ten years, then moved to Grinnell, Iowa, where Albert Shaw attended college.

Dr. Shaw's first wife was Sarah Colborn; their children were G. M. Shaw, Jr., and Lucy. He married Susan Fisher before he left Indiana and their children were Mary and Albert.

The Daniel Wilkins House
by Clara Wilkins Irwin

It was almost a century ago (1845) that my grandfather, Daniel Wilkins, Jr., began the two years task of building his eight-room brick house. True to the tradition of the pioneers of our country, the farm was required to furnish the material from which the house was to be constructed. Back in the hill a limestone quarry was opened from which the big blocks of stone for the basement and foundation walls came. A field not far from the prospective house contained a clay knoll and from this my grandfather and his young son of 12 or 13, with whatever help they could get, shaped and burned bricks, not only for this house, but also for the Isaac McClelland house up the road and some which were used in the Congregational Church ten years later.

Great logs were cut from the native forest and hauled over trails through the woods and across unbridged streams by ox teams to a sawmill along the Miami River to be worked into joists, studding and rafters. Misfortune in the form of a flood intervened when the hardwood (oak?) which had been left at the mill to be cut into flooring was washed away. As it would require considerable time to cut, season and saw more of the same quality, they purchased yellow pine flooring rather than to delay building.

My grandfather, in his customary manner of exactness, left nothing to be desired in sturdiness, quality of material or workmanship. He had the first floor walls built three bricks thick (lying side by side), which is thirteen inches. The upper half was two bricks thick, giving that part a thickness of more than eight inches. The inside walls were built just as thick as the outer walls.

My father knew the number of bricks used in building the house because he learned his arithmetic at his father's knee. My grandfather's favorate problem was to require his pupil to measure the dimensions of the walls, the openings and their sizes, and then apply the rules of arithmetic and figure the number of bricks. This problem extended over some days of time and required enough mental exertion so that when he had finished it to the satisfaction of my grandfather (who knew all the answers through first-hand experience), my father never forgot the numbers.

Grandfather, with his love of accuracy, had his house set squarely north and south, so that the sun at 12 o'clock, sun time, would shine directly in at the south door, thereby enabling him to tell time without the aid of a sundial in a day when time-pieces were less plentiful than now and other agencies for learning the time were yet undreamed.

The house is L-shaped with an in-porch facing north. The front door is to the east and opens to a narrow hall with rooms approximately 16 by 18 feet on either side. Behind the south room is a dining room of the same dimensions and behind this is a one-story kitchen and pantry. The three rooms on the second floor are like those on the first.

Even skilled architects make mistakes in planning houses and I suppose my grandparents talked of and planned for their new house alone. In all probability they did not have access to plans, advice or help and yet in most respects they planned wisely. Many homemakers have looked with envy upon my grandmother's house with its eleven built-in closets. There were two closets in each of the five large rooms, one on either side of the fireplace. The sixth, without a fireplace, had only one closet. Four of the fireplaces were of medium size but the fifth, in the dining room, which served also as kitchen, living room and study hall, was quite large and was provided with a crane. For a long time this fireplace served as a heating system as well as for cooking the food for a large family. It was a number of years after the house was built before the first crude cookstove was purchased.

No room had less than two windows and one had as many as four. There were two stairways but the rooms to which each led were not connected by any door. The stair from the front led to the rooms occupied by the family, while the other ascended from the dining room to the room above for the "hired hands." The uncertain character of many of these persons was considered in planning for the comparative isolation of this room.

It must have been that the kitchen of a farm home in my grandparents' day was less the center of family interest than it is today. It would have been difficult to assemble a family of eleven in a 9 by 16 foot kitchen. However, the cooking was done in the fireplace, meals were eaten in the dining room and there were three spinning wheels upstairs to be kept going, which doubtless accounts in some measure for the lack of importance of the kitchen in the house plan. My grandmother did not have in her kitchen a sink, a cabinet, a refrigerator, two tables and two stoves. She was satisfied with a table, a corner cupboard and a "safe" for food. The pantry, besides its storage space, had three large bins whose slanting lids of walnut were hinged about eight inches from the wall so leaving a nice shelf.

It was no small trip to "run to the cellar" for lard, butter, milk, potatoes, apples, or a slice from one of the big cheeses stored there, because the cellar was under the front part of the house. From the kitchen one must pass through the length of the dining room, across an open porch, into the front hall and down a steep flight of stairs under the front stairs. It involved passing through four doors. The outside entrance to this cellar was through a built-up doorway, as if a tiny room were built onto the house at ground level. The cellar itself was walled with stone, floored with concrete over brick, the ceiling lathed and both ceiling and walls plastered and finished just as they were over the rest of the house. Iron bars insured security when, as in summer, the windows were open.

The attic was a half story running across the front of the house with two small windows in each gable. Only the middle part was floor and the rafters sloped down the sides until they met the joists at a shadowy angle.

Grandfather's house has sheltered four generations of the family, Daniel Wilkins, Jr., who married Eliza Shields. Both were born in 1810; they were married on March 6, 1832.

Their nine children were:

James S. (m. Emeline Miller).
Clarinda (m. John Langridge).
Sarah.
Elizabeth (m. James Tweedy).

Maria; d. aged 21.
Ann.
Parthena (m. Michael Jones).
John (m. Hattie Belle Brosey).
George (m. Jessie Rothermel).

The children of George, the third generation, are:
Clara E. (m. Raymond Irwin).
Elma.
Amy I. (m. Bryan Butterfield).
Sadie M; d. aged 7.

The house is now occupied by Amy and Bryan Butterfield and their five children.

The M. C. Morris House
by Edith Morris

This house stands on State Route 126, one mile southeast of the village, and was built by Elijah Butterfield. In the long-ago year of 1815 there was born to Jeremiah and Polly Butterfield, who lived on the state road just west of Venice, a son, Elijah. In a few years he was attending the special school, conducted in Paddy's Run by the Rev. B. W. Chidlaw. From among his schoolmates he chose Mary Jones, daughter of Maurice and Ann Jones, for his wife and they were married in 1837. The Jones farm lay on the extreme west side of Ross Township, a portion of it, extending across the future Cincinnati-Brookville pike to the township road, became the farm of Mr. and Mrs. Butterfield.

In 1855 Mr. Butterfield erected a new house of brick. Like others of its day, he decided to burn the brick for his dwelling. A kiln was made in the field to the west, now a pasture near the Morgan Township line. A number of extra men had to be employed and fed to carry on this task of burning the brick. His wife persuaded him to journey to Cincinnati and buy a cook-stove, then a new invention, to lighten her labor of cooking for these extra men.

When the first kiln of brick was burned he sold it to a good advantage to meet the expenses of the enterprise. Upon the sale of the brick Mr. Butterfield deposited the money in one of the three banks then in Cincinnati. Tradition says that upon returning home at night he dreamed that the bank had failed and his money had been lost; he dreamed this for three successive nights, whereupon he hurried to the city and withdrew the money, which he brought home safely. Two days later the bank did fail.

A second kiln of brick now was burned for the construction of their own house. Today, in a rainy season, the site of the kiln can be located by the water standing in the depression almost in the center of the pasture, directly in front of the house. The house faces the southwest, about one hundred feet from the highway. It was built for service and durability and the splendid manner in which it has stood constant use and the stress of nearly one hundred years bears evidence that the builders built well. The original structure comprised two full stories, three rooms on each floor, a large hall and open stairway and a porch on the south side. The foundation is of native limestone, two feet thick and eight feet deep. The outside walls and the inside dividing walls which extend from the basement to the attic are solid brick, fourteen inches thick.

One entered the house from stone steps through a large front door, with a nine-inch transom and side glass which admitted much light into the hall. From this hall, nine feet and six inches wide, one entered a large room on each side, fifteen feet and six inches by fourteen feet and six inches, with ten-foot ceilings.

An open stairway with a graceful turn led to the corresponding rooms on the second floor. From the room at the north one entered the third large first-floor room, from which a closed stairway led to the room above. A porch to the south was enclosed on two sides by the ell formed by the house walls.

Each room in the house had a fireplace, two windows, one or two large cupboards. Variation in the appearance and size of these cupboards broke the monotony of the style in each room. The mantle over the fireplace in the south front room was painted in a marbled design, seldom to be found today.

The woodwork in the house is not uniform throughout; walnut, some pine, and occasionally cherry is used. The high ceilings make effective the broad window and door casings which are Etruscan in design; over the doors are wide transoms. All the floors are pine, six inch boards, tongue and grooved. All of the joists and joining timbers are white oak. The well ventilated basement, seven feet deep, furnished storage room for great bins of apples, potatoes, and other provisions of those early days. This basement was reached from the inside by a closed stairway from the first floor and from the outside by broad steps of native stone.

In 1881 Minter C. Morris, whose home was the adjoining farm on the north, purchased the Butterfield farm and to this house brought his young bride, Anna Chidlaw. In this house now was established a new home; they named it "Bryntirion," after an ancestral home in Wales.

The house took on a new meaning—for one must live with a house to understand it, and after a few years Mr. and Mrs. Morris gave expression to the meaning their home had taken on for them, by remodeling to some extent the old structure, and adding six more rooms, which were built along the same lines as the early dwelling. Outside shutters and three verandas were added. This, together with the addition of modern conveniences, lighting, heating and water systems, as they became available, constitute the house today.

This house became a home in every sense of the word; here were found the traditions which were the foundations of the community, religion and education, here were united two pioneer families of the Miami valley. Anna Chidlaw was the daughter of the Rev. B. W. Chidlaw, respected and beloved minister, and the granddaughter of Ezekiel Hughes, pioneer settler of the Miami valley. M. C. Morris was the eldest son of Griffith and Mary Jane Wasson Morris. In that house were reared four sons: Minter Crawford, Walter, Minor and Homer.

Griffith Morris was the second son of Evan and Jane Morris, who came from Montgomeryshire, North Wales, in 1818, and settled in Ross Township. Evan Morris, Sr.'s name appears in 1823 on the first tax duplicate made in Butler County. To this home were born eight children—Evan, Jr., Griffith, John, Mary, Jane, Ann, Mary Ann, and Hannah.

Minter and Anna C. Morris loved their home as they loved their children: Edith, Mary Louise (Mrs. Leslie M. Clawson),

Benjamin Chidlaw and Crawford Minter. They believed that making a home was a matter of both leisure and affection; they filled their home with agreeable things and always found leisure to devote to the interests and pleasure of their children and their friends. Hospitality always prevailed in the home. The devotion of Minter and Anna Morris to their home, their church and their community will forever be an inspiration to their children and to all those who knew them.

The Abner Francis House

When he came to Paddy's Run in 1802, David Francis bought from the government a half section of land in Hamilton County south and west of the Wilkins farm. Whether unsatisfied with this holding because of its distance from the church or the village there is no means of knowing, but in 1812 he purchased in addition to this Hamilton County land, 112½ acres in section 31, Ross Township, from John Matson, who held title from the government, and in 1817, twenty-five acres more of this same Matson land from Hugh Cone. This second purchase must have been to obtain an outlet to the road. Some time after 1817 he built a brick house and a large frame bank barn. The house must have been finished in walnut for there were pieces of walnut finish in a log corn-crib near-by. In 1827 he bought 64 acres adjoining on the east from Squire John C. Jones.

David Francis died in 1848 leaving to his daughter, Elizabeth, the east 89 acres of these purchases and to his grandson, Abner Francis, the west 112½ acres. In September, 1856, Abner Francis bought from his aunt the acres she had inherited from her father and on Christmas of that year Abner Francis and Martha Vaughan were married.

They began housekeeping in the log house on the newly-purchased land. In this house Mary C. and Betsy, daughters of Squire John C. Jones, had been born and here the first Francis child, William, named for his grandfather Vaughan, was born.

While the new house was being planned (in order to get a more satisfactory fronting on the pike) Mr. Francis sold the triangular corner of his land on the opposite side of the turnpike to John Evans in 1857 and bought from John Evans a triangular piece of woods which extended in front of the projected house on his side of the turnpike. This purchase permitted the entrance for the driveway to be on the side towards the village. The ash tree just at the side of the yard gate near the apex of these triangles was a small tree at that time and is now a spreading giant.

One of the workmen on the house was a water-witcher and in a period of rest he located a spot in the yard about 100 feet from the house which he guaranteed would produce abundant water. Mr. Francis, however, was firm and had the well dug about eight feet from the edge of the side porch and close to the kitchen. It was dug to a depth of 36 feet, has a temperature of about 58 degrees F. winter and summer and has never failed in the eighty-eight years of its service.

The house wall is two bricks thick with no space between the two layers of bricks. The perfect bricks from the grandfather Francis' house were utilized as the inner layer.

The plan is slightly modified Colonial with central staircase, hall, parlor, living room, one bedroom, and directly behind the hall, the dining room from which the spiral back stairs ascend and the cellar stairs descend. Back of the dining room is the kitchen.

There are four bedrooms upstairs and an attic above, not fully floored toward the front, but containing the wonders of the world as far as childish memories go. In the days when side-saddles were kept in the attic, one of the hired girls sometimes walked in her sleep. If ever, dreaming of home, she started to bring her side-saddle down the twisting back stairs, the racket raised the whole house to wake and rescue her from her sleep-walking.

The finish of the parlor, hall and sitting room is oak and that of the dining room and upstairs walnut. Heating was by fireplace in the living room and grates in the parlor and front bedrooms upstairs. While a fireplace does not give the uniform heat of the modern furnace, it is much more companionable than a mass of iron in the cellar, and to be able to tend the backlog and fore-sticks day-in and day-out serves as quite a start towards a liberal education.

This house has been home not only to the eight Francis children but also to the six, either left there or sent back from China by Mark Williams, Mr. Francis' half-brother.

Children of Abner Francis, born February 18, 1829; died October 22, 1894, and Martha Ann Vaughan Francis, born November 12, 1832; died February 16, 1905, are:

William, b. February 17, 1858; d. March 13, 1933.
David, b. July 8, 1859; d. August 14, 1943.
John, b. February 15, 1862.
Mark, b. March 19, 1863; d. June 25, 1936.
Eliza, b. December 30, 1865.
Mary, b. November 12, 1868.
Edward, b. March 27, 1872.
Annie, b. October 6, 1873.

Children of Mark and Isabella Williams, either left with Mr. and Mrs. Francis, or sent back from China to their care are:

Henrietta B., b. September 25, 1867; d. May 30, 1898.
Stephen R., b. August 22, 1870.
Emily D., b. May 26, 1873.
Mary E., b. August 3, 1875.
Margaret L., b. May 30, 1878.
Anna L., b. May 30, 1878.

Many of the grandchildren have enjoyed its privileges also. One young person visiting there said afterward, "I never realized that a family as a whole could make the work which had to be done so much like play as these people do."

The original careful planning of the house has made it possible by minor readjustments to modernize the heating system and by borrowing from room and closet space to install toilet and bath.

When the house was built, windows with sash weights were new and expensive, so the windows upstairs were furnished with the older spring peg type of holding the raised sash. This as you may not know, sometimes slips and Mrs. Francis said that the number of panes of glass broken by jarring must have cost much more than the money saved on sash weights.

In 1883 the windows were screened and the wire dishcovers for food on the table and the person detailed to keep the peacock feather flybrush moving over the table at mealtimes all lost their jobs. Incidentally, these screens were placed on the inside of the window sash, not outside, and the original wire screening, although over sixty years old, is still doing service.

It is hard to talk about a house. This really brings to one's mind the picture of the two generations of people who have lived in this frame.

APPENDIX

APPENDIX I

WORLD WAR ONE

The Service Flag of World War I carries the following names:

William Davies	Jerry Moore
Alexander Rae Robinson	Earl M. Rothermel
Chaplain Evan Walter Scott	Perley Evans
Lieut. Hally M. Scott	Gordon Starr
Lieut. Burkert Clark, M. C.	Claude Martin
Clarence M. Scheering	James Hall
Elwyn Martin	

WORLD WAR TWO

Roster of enlisted men March 10, 1945. Honor Roll. Church yard.

Appleton, James C.	McDuffey, Joseph B.
Ashley, Frank	Morehouse, Edward
Buell, Marvin	Morris, Herbert
Casteel, Edward	Morris, Myron J.
Cochran, Lawrence	Morrison, J. Newell
Colt, Robert	Myers, Percy
Cormican, Robert	Owsley, Arnold
Davies, Hugh J.	Phillips, Henry V.
Dees, John	Schneider, Gordon
Eicher, Robert	Scull, Harold
Elstun, Maurice	Spaulding, Robert
Eschenbrenner, David	Spaulding, William
Eschenbrenner, Ralph	Spencer, Clarence
Gildersleeve, John	Spencer, Russell
Hagan, Floyd	Staarman, Charles
Hargis, Vernon	Staarman, Mattheu
Hollowell, Floyd	Starr, Scott
Krause, Charles	Wert Harlan
Lewe, Kenneth	Wert, James C.
McConnell, Lester	West Robert A.
McCreadie, Edwin	Wilmer, Stanley
McCreadie, Roy	Wilson, Albert
McCreadie, Willard	Yater, Kenneth
McDuffey, Charles	Yater, Robert

Maurice Elstun, b. Kent, England, 1917. Miami University, 1940. Entered Army that year, finished bomber school as lieutenant, Midland Field, Texas, June, 1942, m. Evelyn Ross of Uhrichsville, O., went overseas in September, 1942. Served over occupied France, in Africa, and Italy. Advanced in rank to Major; home holidays of 1943. Now stationed in Florida.

Earl Francis Colborn, b. June 15, 1886. Miami University, 1907. Major, Air Corps, 1943. In department of travel and insurance. Service in India. Now stationed in Cincinnati.

Virgil Eugene Happ; gunner's mate on convoy work.

Lieutenant Hugh Jones Davies, co-pilot on a B-24 Liberator, after more than thirty missions was listed as missing in combat over Germany in August, 1944. He was liberated from prison during the advance of the Allies into Germany in May, 1945.

APPENDIX II

THE ARTICLES OF FAITH, CONSTITUTION AND HISTORY
of the
CONGREGATIONAL CHURCH
OF WHITEWATER, MORGAN TOWNSHIP,
BUTLER COUNTY, OHIO

Collected by B. W. Chidlaw in his pastorate and printed by Wm. C. Howells, 1840, the father of W. D. Howells

Art. 1st. We believe that the scriptures of the Old and New Testaments are given by the inspiration of God and are the only infallible rule of faith and practice. Isa. viii 20. 2 Tim. iii 16-17.

Art. 2d. That there is one living and true God, the creator and ruler of the universe, existing in a divine and incomprehensible Trinity, God the Father, Son and Holy Ghost, each possessing divine perfections. Deut. vi 4. 1 Cor. viii 4, 6. 1 Thes. i 9. 1 John v 7. 2 Cor. xiii, xiv.

Art 3d. In the fall of our first parents from their original righteousness and true holiness, and the consequent apostacy, depravity, and lost condition of all the human race, and that all mankind would remain in this sinful condition, till they fell under the just displeasure of God into endless misery; without the grace of God in Jesus Christ. Eccl. vii 29. Rom. iii 23. Eph. 2 1. Rom. v 12-8, 3. Ps. li 5.

Art. 4th. In the incarnation, death, and atonement of Jesus Christ the Son of God, and that salvation from sin is secured only by faith and repentance, that nothing which the sinner can do or suffer will justify his soul before God, and that the imputation of the righteousness of Jesus Christ received by faith is the only ground of his justification, and divine acceptance. John v 14. Phil. ii 8. Rom iii 25, 26 and 5. 6. John iii 16 and 11, 26. Tit. iii 5. 7.

Art. 5th. In the necessity of a radical change of heart, effected through the truth, by the agency of the Holy Ghost—that this change is the commencement of a new and spiritual life, which is carried on by the same divine agent to sanctification and glorification. John iii 7. Titus iii 5. Ezk. xxxvi 27. 2 Thes ii 3.

Art. 6th. That the moral law (Exod. xx chap.) is binding on all mankind as a rule of life, and that obedience to it is a proper evidence of a change of heart. Math. v 6-22. 37, 40. 1 John 2, 3, 5.

Art. 7th. That the sinner is voluntary in his sin, and in the rejection of the Gospel, and if lost, will be his own destroyer. Hos. xiii 9, John v 40.

Art. 8th. That there will be a general resurrection of the dead, and a future judgment, that the righteous shall go into everlasting life and the wicked into everlasting punishment. Acts xxiv 15, 17. 31. 1 Cor. xv. 2 Cor. v 10. 2 Thes. i 9. Math. xxv.

Art. 9th. That Christ has appointed Baptism and the Lord's Supper, to be perpetual ordinances in his church, that infants and adult believers are proper subjects of Baptism, and that the ordinance is scripturally administered by sprinkling or pouring water, that hopeful piety is a qualification for partaking the Lord's supper. Math. xxviii 19, 26, 27. Mark vii 10, 13, 16. Acts ii 38, 41 and xvi 13.

CONSTITUTION

1st. This Church of Jesus Christ shall be called the Congregational Church of Whitewater.

2nd. The Church shall consist of those persons only who are, in the judgment of charity, partakers of a new nature, and walk agreeably to the word of God.

3rd. In our principles of church government, we hold that Jesus Christ is the head and law-giver of the Church, and that in all matters of government and discipline the Church is bound to follow the gospel rules, and that each independent church is competent to transact all its business, and amenable to no ecclesiastical authority, but to its Great Head.

4th. That the officers of the Church, are a minister and deacons chosen by the members of the Church, and set apart to their proper work, the former by the laying on of hands by ordained ministers, and the latter by the Church in solemn prayer.

5th. In the choice of a minister not less than two thirds of the members of the Church shall concur, and, except in cases of proven immorality, not less than two thirds shall procure his dismission. Contracts between the minister and the church shall be renewed every year. Three months notice of a change must be given on either side. But in cases of proven immorality in the minister, the church shall be released from all pecuniary contracts with him from the time of the proofs thereof.

7th. As the special glory of a gospel church consists in the faithful exercise of wholesome discipline, it shall be the duty of the Church to watch over its members in love, and to follow in case of offence the rule of our Lord and Master found in Matt. xviii 15, 16.

8th. The church shall meet on every Saturday before the first Sabbath in every month, unless otherwise ordered by the members, when the special business of the church shall be transacted, and a faithful record shall be kept by a clerk chosen from among the brethren, and that every member shall consider it an important duty to attend the church meetings.

9th. The receiving of members, the exercise of discipline, and all other business not before specified shall be decided by a majority of the members present.

10th. Every candidate for admission into the church shall appear at the church meeting, and having communicated his religious experience, his case shall be subject to the decision of the members present.

11th. Any member in good standing, on application to the church, may receive a certificate of membership and dismission.

12th. Members from other evangelical churches may be received on certificate, providing their papers are not over a year old.

13th. Any member living within the bounds of the congregation, neglecting public worship, and absenting himself from the Lord's table for a longer period than six months successively, shall be visited by the officers of the church, and if no reasonable excuse be given for such absence, he shall be summoned before the church, and if the church is not satisfied with his conduct, his case shall be determined by a majority then present.

14th. The Church shall not proceed against an absent member on the presumption of his guilt. When any member is charged with immoral and unchristian conduct, the clerk, being authorized by the officers of the church, shall notify the said member to appear before the church at the ensuing church meeting or any other time appointed for the purpose. The clerk shall also give a written copy of the charges, and the accused may authorize him to summon such witnesses as may be necessary. Every such case of discipline shall be entered upon liberally in the fear of God, and with fervent prayer for the divine instruction. If the said member after the above citation shall neglect or refuse to appear before the church, then they may try him as if he were present and decide his case immediately.

15. Two-thirds of the members at a meeting, notified a month before hand, agreeing thereunto may at any time alter this constitution.

HISTORY

The origin and early history of this church, planted in the wilderness, fostered by Divine care, and watered by the Divine blessing, are lasting memorials of the truth and faithfulness of God. In the year 1802, the Rev. J. W. Brown, from England, preached for the first time in this neighborhood. His labors extended over a wide territory embracing the counties of Hamilton and Butler. This pioneer of the cross faithfully proclaimed the gospel—and multitudes attended his ministry. The early settlers, generally, attended to the preached word. Mr. Brown's first labors in these vicinities were on the Dry Fork, of Whitewater, Lee's Creek and Paddy's Run.

On July 23, 1803, at the house of D. Lee on Lee's Creek, several of those that attended his ministry, who had (some from Europe, others in the old States,) been members of christian churches, became anxious for the formation of a Church. A committee, J. W. Brown, Asa Kitchel, Andrew Scott, Joab Comstock and David Cunningham, were selected to draft a constitution and lay it before the people. These brethren were of different religious persuasions, but to promote public good and the glory of God, they sacrificed personal predilections, met on the broad basis of christian love, and drew up a confession of faith, and rules of discipline, which after mature deliberation were adopted at a public meeting by those that had first given themselves to the Lord at other places. The church was properly organized September 3, 1803, at the house of John Templeton, on Dry Fork, and called the Congregational Church of Whitewater; Benj. McCarty, Asa Kitchel, Joab Comstock, Andrew Scott, and Margaret Bebb, constituted the church thus organized. In the fall of 1803, Ezekiel Hughes and wife, William and Ann Gwilym, lately from the Congregational church of Llanbrynmair, North Wales, united with the Church. March, 1804, at the house of John Bennefield, J. W. Brown was ordained and accepted the Pastoral care of the infant church. Joab Comstock and Asa Kitchel were chosen and set apart to the offices of Deacons. In the fall of 1804, David and Mary Francis, late from Wales, then residing on Paddy's Run, united with the Church, and preaching commenced in this vicinity. Several families opened their doors for preaching, and were the honored instruments in introducing the gospel into the neighborhood.

Mr. Brown resided in Cincinnati where he published "The Liberty Hall" newspaper. He continued his labors in the church until his death, which took place in 1814 (?) near the Little Miami River, as he was going to an appointment. His unexpected death was a great loss to the church and the community in general. He was a very laborious minister and a good man and died universally lamented.

The records of the church from 1810 to 1815 are lost. Some of the members went to other churches, some left for the beggarly elements of the world, but a few remained steadfast, met together from house to house for prayer and praise, and the Lord blessed them. This was a gloomy period in the history of the Church—but those that waited for the consolation of Israel failed not, their hopes were centered in a covenant-keeping God, and they were not forsaken.

APPENDIX 171

In 1817, the Rev. Rees Lloyd, minister of the Welsh Congregational Church, Ebensburg, Pennsylvania, visited Paddy's Run, and at the request of the Church, became their pastor in December of the same year. Mr. Lloyd preached in Welsh and English, his congregations were large, and many turned to the Lord. The meetings were held at the houses of Ed. Bebb, Dry Fork; Joab Comstock, Wm. Gwilym and John Vaughan.

In 1820 the Rev. Thomas Thomas, from England, came into the neighborhood and commenced his labors as co-pastor with Mr. Lloyd. For some time the church prospered, peace and prosperity prevailed—but in 1822 the Church was divided, some went with Paul and others with Apollos. Mr. Lloyd resigned the pastorship of the church, and Mr. Thomas was chosen sole pastor. In 1823, Mathias Ollis and Roger Sergeant were chosen Deacons and set apart to their proper work.

Public worship was held at the houses of Ed Bebb and John Vaughan, a schoolhouse of Mr. Thomas', and a wagon-maker's shop, near the place where the meeting house now stands.

In 1825 the Brick meeting house, 43 by 30 feet, was erected on a piece of ground given by John Vaughan. At that period this was an arduous but important undertaking, accomplished with no little difficulty.

In 1828, the Rev. T. Thomas, in consequence of various difficulties, resigned the pastoral care of the church. In 1831 he died while pastor of the Presbyterian church at Venice, Ohio. Mr. Lloyd continued to reside in the vicinity, and died in peace at his residence, May, 1839, aged 80.

June, 1828, the Rev. T. G. Roberts of Ebensburg, Pennsylvania, received and accepted a call from the church. Under his ministry, preaching Welsh and English, the work of the Lord prospered and the church increased in numbers. In 1829 David Francis and David Jones were chosen Deacons. The health of Mr. Roberts failed and he was under the necessity of resigning his charge, and of returning home, highly esteemed by all that knew him; where he still survives, though in very feeble health.

In the year 1833, the Rev. E. Roberts of Steuben, New York, took the pastoral charge of the church, but in less than a year, an act of immorality destroyed his usefulness, and the church for the fourth time in thirty years was left without a shepherd. In 1836, John Mering and Hugh Williams were chosen Deacons. After the Rev. E. Roberts left, the Presbyterian ministers in the neighborhood and from Oxford were very faithful in preaching and administering the ordinances.

May 26, 1836, the Rev. B. W. Chidlaw, having received a call from the church, was ordained by the Oxford Presbytery, of which he was a licentiate. He still retains the pastoral care of the church, preaching in Welsh and English—the congregation large—the interest of Zion prospering—peace and love prevailing. The present number, in communion, is about 140. Within the present year 42 have been added to the church. The cause of Sabbath Schools is flourishing, and doing great good. All the other benevolent societies of the age share the prayers and contributions of the church.

October, 1840.
W. C. Howells, Printer,
Hamilton, Ohio.

APPENDIX III

AN HISTORICAL SKETCH OF PADDY'S RUN, BUTLER COUNTY, OHIO.

Delivered Saturday, July 30, 1876, by Rev. B. W. Chidlaw

In the spring of 1795 the good ship Maria, of Salem, Mass., left the port of Bristol, England, bound for Philadelphia. On board was a company of Welsh emigrants. After a tedious passage of thirteen weeks, the ship reached her destination. Some of the emigrants found employment in and around Philadelphia, others passed on to Cambria County, Pennsylvania, and laid the foundation of a large settlement amid the pines and laurel of the Allegheny Mountains. Others, more adventurous, found their way to the gates of the North West Territory at Redstone, Old Fort, and thence descended the Monongahela and the Ohio rivers to the new settlements in the valley of the Miami.

In 1796 Ezekiel Hughes and Edward Bebb, of Llanbrynmair, North Wales, landed at Cincinnati, and spent some time in exploring the new country. The land west of the Miami was not yet surveyed, and until it should be brought into market, Hughes bought 100 acres on Blue Rock Creek on the east side of the Miami, opposite to where the village of New Baltimore now stands. Here they were joined by William Gwilym and his wife who followed them from Red Stone.

When the U. S. land was offered for sale in 1801, Ezekiel Hughes bought two sections in what is now Whitewater township, Hamilton County, and Edward Bebb bought a half section on the Dry Fork of Whitewater, in what is now Morgan township, Butler County. This was the first land bought in the township. On the land of his choice Edward Bebb found a squatter named Aaron Cherry, who two or three years previously had built a cabin and cleared a truck patch. The owner of the soil proposed to pay the squatter for his improvements. This honest fair dealing surprised the squatter—it was a new thing in his roving life as a frontiersman. The offer of payment being made and accepted, Aaron Cherry said: "This is the thirteenth time I have squatted, and it is the first time I was ever offered any pay for my improvements." The generosity of Edward Bebb made Aaron Cherry thenceforth his trusty friend. This man had a family of sons, celebrated in early times for their horse stealing propensities. One of them met his death when pursued for his crimes. He was a leader of a gang of horse thieves, a terror to the settlers, and refusing to surrender, was shot and died in a few days.

After buying land, Mr. Bebb returned to Ebensburg, Pennsylvania, and married Mrs. Margaret Owens (formerly Roberts) of Llanbrynmair. This long journey he performed on foot, but his toil was well rewarded in the prize secured. With his young bride he at once left for his western home. Their son, William Bebb (afterward Governor of Ohio), born December 8th, 1802, was the first white child born in the township. Edward and Margaret Bebb, the first actual settlers, were pillars in society; the latchstring of their cabin always hung out and all new comers received a cordial welcome and timely aid. Mr. Bebb died June 18, 1840, aged 72 years, and Mrs. Bebb, December 3, 1851, aged 77 years, and their graves are among us marked by the loving hands of their sons and daughters, faithful in their testimony of the useful, happy and prolonged life of their honored parents.

William and Morgan Gwilym, brothers from Cevnamam, South Wales, after spending some time at Red Stone, Pennsylvania, came down the Ohio, landed at Cincinnati in 1798 and lived on Blue Rock near their friends Hughes and Bebb.

While at Red Stone, now Brownsville, Pennsylvania, they aided in manufacturing the first iron made west of the Allegheny Mountains. William Gwilym was married to Ann Rowlands of Llanbrynmair, North Wales, and in her found a true woman and a faithful wife. Their (second) daughter Rachel (now Mrs. Davies, an honored resident of Paddy's Run) was born on Blue Rock Creek, now Colerain township, Hamilton County, May 28, 1800, and was the first white child born in that township. In 1802 William Gwilym, who had removed to Paddy's Run, Morgan Township, commenced clearing the forest.

Morgan Gwilym returned to Red Stone and for two years worked at the furnaces. He invested his earnings in a two-horse wagon and iron castings, which were the first brought to this neighborhood. In 1808 he married Elizabeth Evans and theirs was one of the first weddings in the settlement. These two families were as polished stones in the foundation of society in this community. Pioneer hospitality abounded in their log cabins, as well as in their brick dwellings of later times.

William Gwilym died in 1848, aged 82 years, and his wife in 1838, aged 74 years. Morgan Gwilym died in 1845, aged 76 years, and his wife in 1862, aged 78 years.

Andrew Scott and wife settled at the mouth of Paddy's Run about this time. John Vaughan from North Wales bought a half section and settled on it in 1802. He was a man of quiet spirit and a kind heart. Mr. Vaughan built the first frame barn and the first brick house in the settlement, and they remain though built in 1816. He was industrious and enterprising and his influence for good was widely diffused. He died in 1848, aged 83 years.

David Francis and his wife Mary, after remaining some time near Philadelphia, came west, walking to Pittsburgh, then traveling on a "broad horn" down the Ohio to Cincinnati and settling on Paddy's Run. He purchased the choice piece of land now owned by his grandson, Abnes Francis, Esq., in 1812. Deacon Francis died in 1848, aged 76 years, and his wife in 1852, aged 78 years.

James Nicholas and his wife, Mary, from South Wales, settled in 1803. Mr. Nicholas was the first blacksmith in the neighborhood and built the first sawmill on the Paddy's Run. In 1833 his son, James junior, was one of the first three settlers in Gomer, Allen County, which has been a large and prosperous community of Welsh people. Mr. and Mrs. Nicholas followed their son to Gomer in 1834, but Mr. Nicholas died shortly and was one of the first to be buried in the Pike Run Cemetery. His wife survived him many years, returned to Paddy's Run, died aged 87 years and is buried in the old graveyard.

The Parkinson family, consisting of three brothers, came from Pennsylvania, and bought a half section of land in 1803. The land is now owned by Andrew J. Jones, Thomas F. Jones, and Robert Reese. Maurice Jones and his wife Ann from North Wales bought land and settled on Paddy's Run in the year 1803, and both died of cholera in the year 1834, within three days of each other, much respected and deeply lamented.

During 1803 the families of Jacob Phillis, John and Samuel Harden, Bryson Blackburn, George Drybread, James Howard, and Thomas Milholland settled on Paddy's Run and Dry Fork. Blackburn was a blacksmith. His customers had to find the iron and steel which he hammered into axes, hoes, butcher knives, etc., with a brawny arm and a skillful hand.

In 1804 James Shields, a native of Ireland, educated at Glasgow University, Scotland, emigrated with his family from Virginia and purchased a half section of choice land, on which his posterity still reside. Mr. Shields was a man of intelligence and sterling integrity. He served the public as a Representative in the Legislature for nineteen years. These Assemblies of which he was a member met at Chillicothe, Zanesville, and Columbus. In 1828 he was elected to Congress and served his country with fidelity and returned to his constituents a faithful and honored public servant. Mr. Shields traveled from his home on Paddy's Run to our state capitols and to the federal city on horseback, and doubtless enjoyed the long and sometimes tedious rides. The evening of his life was spent in the quiet and comfort of his home in the bosom of a loving family, when in 1831 he died, aged over 70 years, leaving a good name and inheritance to his twelve children and the example of his life for coming generations.

In 1804 John Halstead, of North Carolina, came to the settlement and bought a half section of land, which is still owned and occupied by his descendants. Mr. Halstead lived to see his eightieth year and died in 1855. Mrs. Halstead, a most exemplary woman and good neighbor, died in 1840, aged 66 years.

Abel and Thomas Appleton with their families settled on the half section of land on which some of their descendants still live. Thomas died in 1845, aged 72 years, and his wife Abigail, aged 70 years, soon after. Abel Appleton died of the cholera in 1834, aged 62 years, and his wife Elizabeth long survived him, departing in peace at the advanced age of 89 years.

From 1806 until the close of the war of 1812, the following families came into the settlement: William Evans and family from North Wales settled on the hill west of Dry Fork. Mr. Evans died in 1822, aged 66 years. William Jenkins and family from Virginia settled on Dry Fork. Mr. Jenkins and his wife died at an advanced age.

Two brothers, King and Alexander DeArmond, natives of Pennsylvania, settled, the one on Paddy's Run and the other on Dry Fork, lived to a good old age, and left a numerous posterity, many of whom are still living in the township. Rev. Michael Bottenberg from Maryland, a minister of the United Brethren Church, a faithful and honored servant of God, also came to the township; many of his descendants are among us today. John Mering, a son-in-law of Mr. Bottenberg, came at the same time, and settled on the land now occupied by his son-in-law, Evan Evans, Esq.

Rev. Hezekiah Shaw, son-in-law of John Halstead, a laborious minister of the gospel, resided in the neighborhood and devoted his time to the service of the Methodist Episcopal Church, traveling extensive circuits, useful and honored in his laborious and self-sacrificing duties as a pioneer herald of the Cross.

William D. Jones from Wales settled near Mr. Shields and opened the first mercantile house in the township. Peter Youmans and his family from New Jersey settled on the farm where he lived for many years, a faithful Christian and a genial neighbor. He died in 1837, aged 60, and Mrs. Youmans in 1874, aged 93 years. Ephraim Carmack from Maryland, brought with him a team of eight horses and a genuine Conestoga wagon. He settled where Robert Reese now lives. He was a natural born teamster and distinguished in his cherished avocation. He was also a "mighty hunter" and seldom returned from his excursions without bringing many trophies of his skill in the chase. He removed with his family to Mercer County and was among the early pioneers in that section. In 1817 Rev. Rees Lloyd and family came from Ebensburg, Pennsylvania, and bought land on the hill between

Paddy's Run and Dry Fork. His life and labors will be considered in the history of the church.

In 1818 a new era of emigration from Wales was inaugurated, and large accessions made to the population and resources of the settlement. During the year the following families, chiefly from Montgomeryshire, North Wales, made this valley their homes: John C. Jones and wife, William Davis and wife (the parents of the distinguished physicians John and William B. Davis, now of Cincinnati), George and Catherine Williams, Evan and Mary Humphreys, Griffith Breese and wife and Humphrey Evans and wife.

Connected with these families were a number of adult unmarried persons, among them Francis Jones, who married Elizabeth Francis; John Evans (still surviving at the age of 81 years), who married Miss Sarah Nicholas; Deacon David Jones, who married Mrs. Mary Humphries; John Swancott, who married Miss Mary Jones; David Davies, who married Miss Rachel Gwilym.

The families of Evan Owens, Evan Davies and Tubal Jones from Cardiganshire, South Wales, were added to the families of the valley at this time. From 1820 to 1830 many emigrants from Wales found their way to Paddy's Run, adding to the religious and industrial prosperity of the neighborhood. Among them were Deacon Hugh Williams from Anglesea, North Wales, who married Mrs. Eliza Gwilym Francis, who is with us this day. Joseph Griffiths and Jane, his wife, with a large family of sons and daughters from Carno, North Wales, who in 1837 removed to Allen County, Ohio. Henry Davis from Ebensburg, Pennsylvania, who married Miss Mary Evans; Thomas Watkins, who married Miss Jane Evans; David Roberts, who married Miss Annie Nicholas; Rowland Jones and wife; John R. Jones, who married Miss Jane Gwilym. (Watkins, Roberts, and James Nicholas jr. in 1833; Davis, Rowland Jones, John R. Jones in 1834 with their families were the pioneer settlers of the Welsh communities in Allen County, Ohio.)

Thus we have endeavored to recall the names of the early pioneer families of Morgan Township, especially of the valley of Paddy's Run —families whose record for industry, frugality, probity, hospitality, patriotism and religion is a rich legacy to their posterity and to the entire community.

The facts and incidents connected with life in the cabin and toil in the clearing are worthy of remembrance. The first settlers were men of sound judgment and clear perception. After selecting the land and entering it at the landoffice, they fixed upon the spot amid the unbroken forest where they would build a cabin, and it is evidence of the wisdom of their selections that in almost every instance the beautiful dwellings adorning the valley and its hillsides are located on the identical spots selected over sixty years ago. After selecting the location for a home, the site was cleared, logs chopped, clapboards rived and the puncheons hewed. The cabin was then raised, all the neighbors assisting; four corner men, expert choppers, on the building, the rest rolling up the logs; men and women uniting their strength kept the corner men busy receiving the logs, chopping the notch and hewing the saddle. Two days finished the job; oil papered windows, doors of clapboards hung on wooden hinges; the floors laid with smooth hewed puncheons; the cracks chunked and daubed; the chimney built of wood and mud—the home of the pioneer was finished and occupied.

The furniture was largely made by the help of the axe, drawing knife and auger, and of whatever articles the settler brought with him or purchased in the village of Cincinnati. The question what shall we eat and what shall we drink they answered by using the articles of subsistence that a kind Providence brought in their way. The forest abounded in game and the river in fish; sugar and honey they obtained from the forest, and their truck patches furnished vegetables; soon their industry enabled them to husk corn and harvest wheat; pork and poultry contributed to their supplies, and their tables were loaded with good things. Instead of "store tea" they had sassafras and spicewood, delicious and aromatic. None ever suffered for want of daily food, and in a few years all the necessaries and comforts of life abounded.

In early times our pioneer ancestors were compelled to use ingenuity as well as invention in providing clothing. Buckskin furnished material for moccasins and fringed hunting shirts, but in a few years sheep were introduced for wool and flax sown; these the women spun, wove and cut, and made substantial and comfortable garments; the bark of trees was used for coloring, and there was no lack of taste or subjection to the tyranny of fashion in the art of dressmaking. Sunbonnets made of pasteboard and a yard of calico were fashionable for forty years.

For several years "blazed" tracks or paths, with the underbrush removed answered the purpose for traveling from cabin to cabin. After the county road had been laid out and opened from Cincinnati to the Miami, and the regions beyond in 1805, and Morgan Gwilym brought the first wagon into the township, a new era of transportation dawned on the new country. For many years the settlers took the produce of their fields, poultry yards and dairies to Cincinnati on pack horses. At an early day, Paddy's Run butter commanded a quick sale and a premium in Lower Market, then the business center of the Queen City.

Hospitality and sociability were cardinal virtues among the pioneers. Their raisings, log-rollings, corn-huskings, and harvestings; their chopping frolics, quiltings, and wool pickings are the memorials of their readiness to help each other. In the absence of a factory, their homemade woolens were fulled by using a trough—a row of men on one side and of women on the other using their feet, the soap and water served a good purpose, and the process was eminently successful.

Whisky made in the one-horse distilleries of the day, free from adulterations, was used on these occasions, but seldom to excess. Some knight of the fiddle being present, the youth wound up the labors of the day with dancing. The "Race Lane" is suggestive of horse racing, and shooting matches, when the best marksman would carry off the turkeys, were the common sports of the day.

The year 1811 was memorable for the appearance of a wonderful comet. During the summer a fearful pestilence visited the settlement and nearly all who were smitten by the disease died. It was called the "cold plague." After the pestilence came a terrible hail storm, the ground was covered with pieces of ice of irregular shape, some of them measuring six inches in circumference. In 1812 an earthquake convulsed the settlement and filled the hearts of the people with terror; many of our older citizens remember the shocks, having felt them in their own persons. These wonderful visitations of Providence produced a marked effect on the people, not of superstitious awe, but a devout acknowledgment of the rulings of Divine Providence.

The Wars of 1812 and 1861-1865

In 1813 a company of volunteers was raised in Morgan Township under the command of Capt. W. D. Jones. The home of John Vaughan was the place of rendezvous. The patriotism and liberality of the settlers was manifested in an abundant supply of blankets and subsistence for the use of the volunteers. They marched with other troops to the relief of General Hull, then beleaguered by the British at Detroit. On their way through the forest they suffered for food; near Fort Wayne, Indiana, they captured three bushels of parched corn in bark boxes secreted by the Indians and on this they subsisted until they reached the fort. Hull having surrendered, they returned. One of their number, Samuel Harding, died of disease contracted in the service.

In 1861 when our national life was imperiled by armed traitors, thirty-eight volunteers from this township enlisted in the 5th O. V. Cavalry, and during the war a large number entered the army, all rendering their county in the time of its need heroic and important service. Some laid down their lives on the battlefield and others have suffered from wounds and disease. The war record of Morgan Township is a noble tribute to the loyalty and heroism of its inhabitants and the names and memory of the brave soldiers should be held in everlasting remembrance.

The first death in the township is said to have been a daughter of Benjamin James, a squatter on Dry Fork, and resulted from the bite of a rattlesnake at the spring. A coffin was made by splitting a black walnut log and dressing it with a broadaxe and drawing knife. These slabs were fastened with wooden pins; the body laid in this rude casket was carried by loving hands to the first grave dug in the neighborhood at the foot of what is now known as "Race Lane." Mrs. Blackburn, mother of William Blackburn, was the first who died on Paddy's Run, and her remains were buried in the woods on the hill west of where Mrs. Margaret Sefton resides. A pen of logs surrounds it and some of us have seen it.

A clock case now owned by Mrs. Mary Vaughan, made for her father, Edward Bebb, by Stephen Hayden in 1804, shows the ingenuity and taste of this pioneer cabinet maker. It is made of cherry slabs, dressed as best he could, overcoming the want of sawmills with a whipsaw. Stephen Hayden with such tools as he had made a beautiful and neatly ornamented clock case worthy of a place in the great Centennial Exhibit at Philadelphia. For over seventy years it has been the cozy home of a brass clock which Mrs. Bebb brought from Wales seventy-nine years ago. The face of the clock is 12 by 12 inches, but when the case was made the Cincinnati market could not furnish a piece of glass large enough to cover it. The glass is in two pieces, neatly joined by the hand of a skillful mechanic. This venerable clock (good as new after all its ticking in four-score years) was a great curiosity to the Indians who frequently visited Mr. Bebb's cabin. He would make the clock strike around in their hearing, but the children of the forest must have the cabin door open, that in case of danger they might seek safety in flight.

Capt. William D. Jones brought the first stock of goods into the township on a pack-horse, and opened a place of business near where the turnpike crosses Paddy's Run. His business was conducted chiefly on a bartering basis, as specie was very scarce.

The first physicians were Drs. Sloan and Millikin of Hamilton and Dr. Crookshank of Harrison. They practiced as early as 1806, and were eminent in their profession and useful in the community.

The township was organized in 1811, but in 1808 Maxwell Parkinson officiated as justice of the peace, but by what authority is unknown —probably appointed by the Governor. After the organization of the township, the citizens elected King DeArmond, William D. Jones, Hugh Smith, William Jenkins, William Bebb, Ephraim Carmack, and others to this office.

The men who laid the foundations of society in these beautiful valleys were intelligent and the firm friends of knowledge. In 1821 a bill was passed in the Ohio Legislature incorporating the "Union Library Association of Morgan Township and Crosby Township." The shares cost $3.00, and sixty-five were taken. The books purchased were standard works on history, morals and science. The library was kept at Smith's Mill on Dry Fork, and the shareholders assiduously improved their opportunities to read.

The Asiatic cholera in a malignant type visited the neighborhood in 1834, especially the eastern side of the valley of Paddy's Run. About sixty persons, mostly adults, died during the prevalence of the epidemic which continued about three weeks. Some families were almost swept away by the power of the deadly pestilence, and there was scarcely a house which the angel of death did not visit. In 1852 the flux prevailed as an epidemic, and in two weeks twenty died of the disease.

On the 16th of November, 1854, a terrible calamity was occasioned by the fall of the steeple of this church. Six valuable lives were lost—Nathaniel Jones and Robert Jones were instantly killed; on the next day John C. Jones, Esq., aged 58, died from injuries received. His death was a great loss to his family, the church and the community. In a month Jacob Phillis, the contractor, died, and after lingering several weeks Thomas Jones and Elias Williamson died.

In 1866 Robert Griffiths and his family, after residing several years on Paddy's Run beloved and respected, left for Missouri. They embarked at Cincinnati on the steamer "Nannie Byers." Near Madison, Indiana, the boat sunk, and this worthy family, father, mother, four adult children and a son-in-law, lost their lives in the turbid waters of the Ohio. Their remains were recovered and buried in the old graveyard, in the presence of an immense concourse of sorrowing friends.

The oldest graveyard in the township was located on the west side of Camp Run near its mouth; all traces of this first burial place are obliterated. John Halstead and Ephraim Carmack opened graveyards on their farms, which the neighborhood used for many years. In 1821, John Vaughan and Morgan Gwilym donated the lot for meeting house and graveyard and until 1867, when the new cemetery was opened, this was the place where the dead found a sepulcher, and where nearly all the old settlers have been buried.

Religious History

Several of the pioneer settlers were members of churches, and all of them respected the Christian religion. They entered these unbroken forests with an open Bible held in high estimation—they honored the Sabbath day and regarded Christianity and its institutions as of first importance in the moral and material prosperity of the settlement. With these convictions they early and kindly opened their cabin doors and cordially welcomed any minister of the gospel whose zeal and faithfulness led him to the neighborhood.

The first minister that unfurled the gospel banner in the settlement was Rev. John W. Browne, of Cincinnati, a Congregationalist from England. He preached at the houses of Edward Bebb on Dry Fork, Andrew Scott at the mouth of Paddy's Run, John Vaughan of Paddy's Run, and David Lee on Lee's Creek. All the settlers through these localities attended and appreciated his ministry.

In July, 1803, at the house of David Lee, a committee consisting of Mr. Browne, Asa Kitchel, Andrew Scott, Joab Comstock, and David Cunningham was appointed to draft a constitution and articles of faith for the proposed religious society and present it before the people.

APPENDIX

On September 3, 1803, at the house of John Templeton on Dry Fork near New Haven, the report of the committee was adopted. The society was called "The Whitewater Congregational Church"; its doctrinal basis evangelical but not sectarian. Its first members were Benjamin McCarty, Asa Kitchel, Joab Comstock, Andrew Scott, Margaret Bebb, Ezekiel Hughes, William and Ann Gwilym, David and Mary Francis. In this little company of believers, as sheep scattered in the wilderness, were members of the body of Christ, his friends and followers from Scotland, Ireland, Wales and New England. One in Christ, they cordially united in Him, and organized a New Testament Church. In 1804, at the house of John Bennefield, in Crosby Township, Hamilton County, according to previous arrangement, Mr. Browne was ordained to preach the gospel and administer the ordinances of the church.

The record shows that the church appointed a committee of its own members to set apart this brother to the sacred office and work of the ministry. The service of ordaining him was simple and in accord with their views of Bible teaching, and recognized as valid as if performed with pomp and show within the walls of a cathedral, by men appointed and vested with authority by church and state. The little flock thus folded, and in the care of the pastor, meeting on the Sabbath from cabin to cabin, and often with a large congregation, worshipping God in the grove beneath the shade of the forest trees, grew and multiplied, and the hand of the Lord was with his people. In 1814 (?) Mr. Browne lost his life in the Little Miami River, on his way to an appointment in Clermont County. His death was a great loss to the church and the community. From 1810 to 1817 the records of the church are lost.

Without a meeting-house and without regular preaching, the church held together, and its influence on the side of morality and religion, of social and intellectual culture continued; its light ceased not to burn. Rev. Rees Lloyd, of Ebensburg, Pennsylvania (who with his wife and children were passengers on the Maria in 1795), was invited to accept the pastorate of the church, to preach in Welsh and English. He entered upon his labors in 1817, preaching in dwelling houses and gathering good congregations. In 1820 Rev. Thomas Thomas, of Welsh parentage, but a native of England, pastor of a Congregational church at Chelmsford, England, emigrated to this country with his family, and was invited as co-pastor with Mr. Lloyd. He was a good scholar, an able expounder of the Holy Scriptures and an eloquent preacher. His labors in this and the surrounding neighborhoods greatly advanced the cause of religion. Mr. Lloyd gave up the pastorate of the church, and Mr. Thomas continued, and also established a school which gained much celebrity. In 1823 Mathias Ollis and Roger Sergeant were chosen deacons.

Mr. Thomas preached in his school room, in dwelling houses, in the wagon-shop of David Jones and when the weather was favorable in the open air, beneath a grove of sugar trees, where Mrs. Eliza Williams now resides. The want of a house of worship was a great necessity, and indeed a hindrance to the permanent growth and spiritual prosperity of the church. The people, led by their pastor, had a heart to work, and in 1823 the old meeting house was commenced, the foundations 43 by 30 feet were laid, and the brick burned. The next year the walls were erected and the building enclosed. In 1825, temporary seats and a pulpit made of two upright scantling and a board furnished the house of the Lord. The first service within its walls was the funeral of Mrs. Ruth Vaughan.

In 1827 Mr. Thomas gave up the care of the church, and accepted a call to the pastorate of the Presbyterian church at Venice, Ohio, where he labored successfully until his death in 1831, and he was buried among his people honored and beloved. Mr. Lloyd also retired from the active work of the ministry, and died in 1838, aged 80 years, and his remains interred in a graveyard adjoining the "Hickory Chapel" near Daniel Otto's house, on the hill between Paddy's Run and Dry Fork. In July, 1828, Rev. Thomas G. Roberts, of Ebensburg, Pennsylvania, entered upon the pastoral office in this church, preaching in both languages. Under his labors the church prospered, but failing health made it necessary for him to return to his home in Pennsylvania in the year 1831. Rev. Evan Roberts, of Steuben, New York, came to the neighborhood, and preached several months, then returned home and died in 1834.

In 1836, Rev. B. W. Chidlaw, of Radnor, Ohio, a student at the Miami University, who had preached in the neighborhood for over a year, was called to the pastorate. He was ordained in May, 1836, Rev. R. H. Bishop, D.D., President of the University, presiding. Rev. Prof. J. W. Scott, D.D., delivered a charge to the people, and Rev. S. Scovill, of Harrison, a charge to the young pastor. Mr. Chidlaw continued his ministry for seven years, the church growing in numbers and spirituality, and the Sabbath School work of the church in the surrounding neighborhoods was greatly extended. He entered the service of the American Sunday School Union and continues in it to this day.

In 1843, Rev. Ellis Howell, from England, entered upon the work of the ministry, and continued several years. He is now pastor of the Presbyterian church at Reily, Ohio. He was followed by Rev. Joseph H. Jones, from South Wales, an earnest, faithful servant of God, now ending a useful and prolonged life in his home in Randolph County, Indiana. Since that time Rev. James W. Pryse, now laboring in Minnesota; Rev. D. W. Wilson, now in Tennessee; Rev. J. M. Thomas, now in Pomeroy, Ohio; Rev. H. R. Price, whose long life and useful ministry closed so recently; Rev. J. C. Thompson and Rev. George Candee, both still living and laboring in northern Ohio, have had the pastoral care of the church. Rev. John L. Davies, a graduate of Marietta

College and a student at Lane Seminary, was ordained by the Conference of Southern Ohio, in Gallia County, and entered upon his work as pastor a few months ago with prospects of success in his important work.

Deacons of the Church

The brethren called to the office of Deacons were men of "honest report, full of the Holy Ghost and wisdom." Their names and services deserve our recall and a warm place in the memory of the present generation. Of Joab Comstock, Asa Kitchel, Matthias Ollis and Roger Sargent, the time of their death, their age and place of burial we have no information. David Francis many of us knew and esteemed highly for his work's sake. He died in 1848, aged 76 years. David Jones, whose recent death the entire community deplores, was a stern, steadfast disciple of the Lord Jesus Christ—a pillar in the church, strong in the faith and faithful in duty.

John Mering and Hugh Williams in the vigor of their days were chosen deacons, and they failed not in the conscientious and faithful discharge of their duties. Brother Mering, by the kick of a horse in his door-yard, was called from the labors of life to the rest of heaven. His sudden death was generally deplored, and his memory is fragrant unto this day. He died in 1849.

Hugh Williams, in his quiet and genial way, showed his love for the church and his interest in its prosperity. A devoted student of the Scriptures, he was rooted and grounded in the faith. He died in peace March 7, 1870, aged 64 years, and left to his family and to the church, the inheritance of a good name and devoted piety.

In 1848 David Davies was elected to the office of a Deacon, and faithfully discharged its duties until his death in 1855, aged 62 years. The same year William Jones received and accepted a call to the Deaconship. He was a man of prayer, mighty in the Scriptures and full of humble devotion to his work. He died in 1858, aged 64 years. John Gibbon served with fidelity in the office of a deacon until he removed to Illinois, where he still resides.

Thomas F. Jones, Abner Francis and Robert Reese are now the acting Deacons of the church, loving Zion and laboring for its prosperity. The members of the church now number one hundred and fifty, and the attendance on the worship of God on the Sabbath is large. The inhabitants of this vicinity have always been distinguished for their observance of the Sabbath, their high estimate and profound reverence for the Holy Bible, and their attendance on the ministry of the Gospel. From the early days when the tabernacle of God was movable, and fondly welcomed into the log cabins of the godly pioneers, the religious element in its purity and power, in moulding the highest type of Christian civilization, has been cherished and supported in this community. The early embodiment of the religious life and character of the original settlers into a church organization, founded on the broad and sure foundation of our common Christianity, has secured innumerable blessings to the generations following. True to its principles of Christian unity and cooperation, intolerance and bigotry blighted not this garden of the Lord. One strong and united church, and not a half dozen sectarian organizations weak and powerless for doing good, is the glory and power of Zion on this hill of the Lord today. With this spirit of love and labor, of wisdom and mutual confidence, they cohered and formed the church whose history abounds in testimonials of the Divine favor and in fulfillment of the promises of a covenant-keeping God. The liberality of the church in building two houses of worship both standing today, in the support of the gospel at home, and in sending it abroad from the time when a part of the salary of the first pastor was paid in grain, delivered at his home in Cincinnati, has never failed.

Liberal bequests were made by Deacon Hugh Williams and William Jones to the American Bible Society and the American Missionary Society. Miss Ann Evans, Deacon David Francis and Mrs. Elizabeth Gwilym have bequeathed a generous sum for the support of the gospel in this church. The fund is safely invested and the interest available for the purposes designed.

The first Sabbath School was organized in 1819, in a private house and superintended by Benjamin Lloyd. The attendance of the youth and adults was good, and much interest excited in the study of the Bible and committing verses to memory. After the arrival of Rev. Mr. Thomas and his family in 1821, a new life was infused into the Sabbath School, and a supply of books published by the American Sunday School Union secured. These books were very generally read and found to be very useful. The school has continued until now and has been very useful to the church and neighborhood. It now numbers one hundred and fifty scholars, with a band of twenty faithful teachers under the supervision of Deacon Abner Francis.

The influence and labor of the pastor, Rev. J. L. Davies, in encouraging the teachers and scholars to study the Scriptures is doing much to elevate the standard and the methods of teaching, and in promoting the general interests of the good work. For over fifty years the Sabbath School with its Divine textbook, its sacred toleration and oral instruction, has been a great blessing to the community. For many years a school held in the old meeting house was conducted in the Welsh language which the adult people greatly enjoyed. As the Welsh language declined the school was given up a few years ago, but the record of its usefulness is treasured on high.

Prayer meetings and church meetings have a history coeval with the church. Every week, generally on Thursday evening, a goodly attendance of adults and youth meet for prayer and praise. For many years a weekly conference, a society meeting, was held in the Welsh language, a blessed means of grace developing and strengthening the religious life and experience of all that attended. A monthly meeting of the church for the transaction of business has been held from the beginning. The sacrament of the Lord's Supper is administered monthly, accompanied with special religious services, rendering the occasion a spiritual privilege highly enjoyed by the church. For many years the female members of the church and congregation have sustained a weekly prayer meeting in the English language, which has awakened a deep religious interest and called out much Christian work in behalf of temperance and every other good work and word.

Church Clerks

The records of the church, embodying much valuable and interesting history, have been kept by the following brethren: James Scott was appointed in 1804, and served many years. From 1820 to 1827 the records are signed by the pastor, Rev. T. Thomas. In 1828, Evan Davies, a faithful common school teacher, was chosen clerk, and continued in office for twelve years until he removed to take charge of the public schools of Hamilton. In 1837 Deacon David Davies was appointed, and served faithfully until he was succeeded by Thomas F. Jones in 1849. Brother Jones, gifted in the use of the pen, kept the records until he was succeeded by Griffith Morris in 1871, who still serves in this office.

The Young Men of Paddy's Run

Rev. Thomas E. Thomas, D.D., graduated at the Miami University, Oxford, Ohio, in 1834, entered the ministry in 1836 as pastor of the Presbyterian church at Harrison, Ohio, afterward at Hamilton and Dayton. He closed his useful life in 1875, when serving the church as professor in Lane Theological Seminary. He was a profound scholar, an able expositor of the Holy Scriptures and an eloquent preacher.

Alfred Thomas graduated at the same University in 1838, entered the profession of law, and now resides in Washington, D. C., where he holds an important position in the law department of the U. S. Treasury.

Rev. Abner Jones, son of Francis Jones, graduated at Oxford in 1858, and at Lane Seminary in 1861. He was pastor of the Congregational church of Columbia, and New Albany, Licking County, Ohio. In 1864 he responded to the call of his country and entered the service as a Christian hero. He died at Alexandria, D. C., and his remains were brought home to rest in the new cemetery.

Rev. W. Mark Williams, son of Hugh Williams, graduated at Oxford in 1858 and at Lane Seminary in 1861. After an acceptable and useful ministry of two years, he with his wife embarked under the auspices of the American Board of Commissioners for foreign missions for China, where he remains in charge of the mission of Kalgan, in the northern part of the empire.

Rev. Thomas McClelland and his brother Samuel, sons of Isaac McClelland, graduated at Oxford. The former is pastor of the Presbyterian church at Chester, Ohio, and the latter doing good service as an educator.

Oliver Jones, son of Deacon Thomas F. Jones, and Griffith M. Shaw, son of Dr. Shaw, graduated at Wabash College, Indiana. Mr. Jones is a successful teacher and Mr. Shaw died in 1873.

Roger Williams, son of Hugh Williams, graduated at Oxford in 1872, went to Europe the following year, lost his health and with much difficulty came home to die. He was preparing for the life of a journalist, but his early death cut off his purposes and his sun went down while it was yet noon.

Several of the young men of the neighborhood without a university education have made their mark in the world in professional life. Among them we note Evan Morris, a civil engineer; the new church was built under his supervision and several important turnpikes show his skill and faithfulness in his profession.

Dr. Griffin Shaw entered the medical profession and was greatly esteemed in the community, and his early death was universally lamented. Murat Halstead, son of Col. Griffin Halstead, has for many years edited the Cincinnati Commercial, one of the leading newspapers of our country. Mr. Halstead is esteemed as one of the first journalists of our land.

Many of the young women of Paddy's Run deserve great credit for their noble ambition to obtain an education, and for the use they have made of their scholarship and talents in their devotion to the work of life in its highest forms of usefulness and true womanhood.

Sketch of the Schools
by Principal James A. Clark

The first school in the township was in a log house built in 1807, on land now owned by Thomas Shields, Esq., and taught by Miss Polly Wiley. Her salary was seventy-five cents a week, boarding around. She taught her twenty scholars reading and spelling. She was succeeded by a Mr. Jenkins in 1808. He was noted for his method of teaching morals and manners to his pupils. Before dismissing them at noon, he collected them with their dinner around a large table in the center of the room, and after asking a blessing upon the meal, he acted as "autocrat of the dinner table," requiring silent attention from all.

In 1809 another school was begun in a rented log cabin on Dry Fork, in the western part of the township. Here Adam Mow taught a subscription school at $1.50 per scholar, for a term of three months.

In 1810 the citizens of this place met together and built a log cabin school house with cat and clay chimney, wooden latch, slab benches, board roof and two small windows; but provided with no blackboard, maps, globe or charts. Here the children were taught to spell in Dilworth's spelling book, and to read the New Testament, Bunyan's Pilgrim's Progress, and American Preceptor, and to write, and to cipher in Bennet's and Pike's arithmetics, graduating at the "rule of three." The qualifications of the teacher were decided by those appointed to employ teachers, according to reputation, or recommendation, or decided characteristics, as good penmanship, ability in arithmetic, or austerity in manner and discipline.

In this way the schools were kept during three or four months of each year, no change being made except a change of teachers occasionally, until 1819, when David Lloyd, a graduate from Philadelphia, was employed to teach. He introduced grammar and geography into the schools, and classified his pupils in these branches and in arithmetic. Before this each pupil recited by himself, or rather did not recite at all. He was an eccentric man, having spent most of his life in a vain effort to invent perpetual motion. He taught for the same wages as his predecessors, and collected his tuition from his patrons.

The general government had made some provision to help the schools before this, by appropriating the land in section sixteen of each township for this purpose. This land was leased for a series of years by the township trustees, to be put under cultivation, and now part of it was rented for one-third grain rent, which amounted to twenty or thirty bushels of corn, worth ten or twelve cents a bushel. This plan of renting the land for grain rent was continued until the land was considerably run down, when most of it was sold, and the interest of the money divided, pro rata, among the schools.

In 1821, in addition to the Common School, Rev. Thomas Thomas, father of the late T. E. Thomas, D.D., of Lane Theological Seminary, established a high school and boarding school, in which he taught for a series of years, advanced pupils in grammar, geography, arithmetic, algebra, and geometry. This was a great impetus to the growth of the educational spirit of the community, and in the same year the "Union Library Association of Morgan and Crosby" was formed and chartered by the Legislature, and approved by the Supreme Court, Judge Burnet and Judge McLain ratifying the articles. In this library were such books as Plutarch's Lives, Rollin's Ancient History, Josephus, Mungo Park's Travels, Lewis and Clark, Campbell on the Miracles, Paley's Evidences of Christianity, Butler's Analogy, etc., and by examining the librarian's record, we find that these books were drawn out and read by almost every citizen of the two townships; and thus the intelligence of the people was greatly increased and a desire for improvement was awakened in both old and young.

And this desire has been growing ever since, so that when the schools were organized under the state law in 1826, the people were eager to avail themselves of its advantages. A new schoolhouse was built, and

William Bebb, who became Governor of Ohio in 1846, was the first teacher employed under the state law. He taught two years and then taught high school four years, when he went to Hamilton and studied and practiced law until he was elected Governor. We had township examiners to decide upon the qualifications of teachers as early as 1825.

The Hon. James Shields, who had been nineteen years a member of the Ohio Legislature, and who was afterwards in 1829 a member of Congress, was the first examiner. Excepting Professor McGuffey, he was perhaps the best scholar and most influential man in the county, taking a leading part in all the educational enterprises. He was educated at Glasgow, Scotland. He examined Governor Bebb, Evan Davies and other noted teachers. From 1828 to 1832, Governor Bebb was township examiner. Evan Davies taught here for six or seven years, commencing in 1830. He was for forty years one of the most prominent educators of Butler County, being County Examiner from 1840 to 1869. After Mr. Bebb, the Rev. Benjamin Lloyd and Rev. B. W. Chidlaw, well known as a veteran worker in the American Sunday School Union and in Ohio as a trustee of the Reform Farm School at Lancaster, Ohio, were township examiners. From 1837 to 1840, Mr. Chidlaw taught high school here with great success.

These eminent teachers gave a good education to those who have since furnished pupils and teachers for our schools. Among the most noted in the Rev. Thomas Thomas' school we might mention Charles Selden, author of Selden's Book-keeping, and the late T. E. Thomas, D.D., of Lane Theological Seminary, who is the author of one of the best works on homiletics in the English language. In Governor Bebb's school we mention William Dennison, who became Governor of Ohio in 1861, Hon. G. M. Shaw of Indiana, and Hon. Daniel Shaw, a member of the first legislature of Louisiana after the late rebellion. He was sheriff of Grant parish and had charge of the colored troops at the time of the Colfax massacre; and the Hon. Peter Melendy, one of the most prominent Republican politicians in Iowa. These schools were patronized by many of the most wealthy families in Cincinnati and the Southern states.

Mr. Evan Davies built up and popularized the common schools and prepared pupils for the high school, teaching some of the higher branches himself in the public schools, so that Mr. Chidlaw's school had more of a home influence. He taught on the modern plan, introducing the modern improvements of blackboards, charts, etc. He prepared some eminently successful teachers, among whom we may mention T. F. Jones, Griffith Morris, Evan Morris, and M. R. Shields. These gentlemen conducted the schools here and in the neighboring villages with great success for several years. Mr. M. R. Shields afterward filled the office of county surveyor very successfully in Butler County for a number of years. Mr. Evan Morris graduated in civil engineering in the College of Cincinnati, under Professor Mitchell, a distinguished mathematician and astronomer. Some distinguished editors also attended Mr. Chidlaw's school, the best known of whom is Murat Halstead, the editor and publisher of the Cincinnati Daily Commercial, whose father, Col. Griffin Halstead, still lives here.

Under the management of these excellent teachers the public schools were very prosperous, and wages were increased from $12 to $25 and afterwards to $30 a month. In 1852 a new library association was formed and about one thousand volumes of choice standard works were purchased for it, which were free to the people to read.

Thus it will be seen that up to this time, this place has shown a praiseworthy example in educational progress. Since this time we have had some ups and downs, and individual failures, such as occur almost everywhere. But it is not our province to speak of these, but rather to show the general progress that has been made. No one should suppose that every teacher has been a success because we do not take pains to point out the failures that have been made, though we feel free to say that these have been few and far between.

In 1858 the academy or high school was organized on a more permanent basis. Twelve of the most prominent citizens were appointed as directors who made themselves responsible for the payment of all expenses connected with the school, the funds for which were mainly derived from tuition, and they employed David McClung, afterwards Judge McClung, as principal, at a salary of $3.00 per day. At this time blackboards, wall maps, globes, charts, instruments and all the modern appliances to facilitate teaching were systematically used. The public school was also at this time divided into two departments, primary and secondary.

The Misses Atherton, three sisters who received their preparatory education here and finished their studies at the Western Seminary at Oxford, and Michael Jones, of this place, were all very popular teachers in the public schools and were employed for several years. In the high school the teachers were changed often, though most of the teachers were men of ability, being nearly all graduates of colleges, and all professional teachers, as the rules of the company required that none but professional teachers should be employed. Yet the colleges had given them good training, and were not at fault, for most of them left their situations here because they obtained better situations elsewhere.

Of the noted teachers we mention two, Rev. David Wilson, who had been a missionary in Syria for fifteen years, a man of great ability and energy and success as a missionary, preacher and teacher, and Rev. Mark Williams, a graduate of Miami University and of Lane Theological Seminary, who has been for the past ten years a missionary at Kalgan, China, sent out by the American Board. He was prepared for college here.

A large number of the principals in the high school here are now filling high professional positions as preachers, lawyers, and doctors.

In 1865 James A. Clark, the present principal of the graded schools, was employed as the principal of the high school. Under his management the school was quite successful, but in order that both the high school and the public school might be more efficient, it was necessary that they should be united, and the people felt this. And so, after the Act of the Legislature, passed April 9, 1867, being an act for the organization of Special School Districts, the leaven of enthusiasm so pervaded the whole community that they were unanimous in their vote to avail themselves of the benefits of this law. And on December 10th, 1869, the New London Special School was organized, and Messrs. Jacob Scheel, Evan Evans, and Thomas Appleton were the first board appointed under this act. They employed as principal Samuel McClelland, a former pupil of the high school, and graduate of Miami University and also a member of the present board of examiners of Butler County. But at this time the school was not thoroughly graded and classified, for want of suitable rooms.

In 1871 a large and beautiful lot of about three acres was purchased, and a commodious brick school house was erected, containing four departments furnished in modern style, the whole costing about thirteen thousand dollars. At that time the basis of the present system of classification was formed by Miss Florence Shafer (the only lady teacher ever employed in the high school) and the three members of the board then acting viz. Messrs. Griffith Morris, Abner Francis, and Evan Evans, the first two being men of more than ordinary scholarship and experience as teachers, and all three men of wealth and influence; and above all thoroughly in earnest in their efforts to build up a good school. Three grades were formed, primary, intermediate and high school.

In 1872 James A. Clark, former principal of the high school, was employed as principal; and since that time much has been done with the co-operation of the board and citizens, to establish a course of study and system of education and mental training that would best prepare our youth for citizenship and the duties of life.

We have had for the past five years an enumeration of about one hundred and ninety pupils of school age in the district, which is two by three miles, the population being about stationary. We have enrolled each year, since 1872, about one hundred and eighty-five pupils, including about twenty pupils each year who attended from other places and who pay tuition at the rate of thirty dollars for forty weeks in the high school. And we could have double the number if we were prepared to accommodate them. A great many pupils attend the high school to prepare for teaching and many young gentlemen and ladies to prepare for college.

It must not be inferred from what has been said of the young men of Paddy's Run that they have surpassed the young women; for as great a number have graduated with honor, and have filled, and are still filling high positions in the work of education and of the church.

Conclusion

The generations yet to come, in the example of their godly ancestors, will have a rich legacy. A good name untarnished—brain and muscle embodied in useful industry, a life of sound morality and true religion is a grand inheritance and worthy of the highest appreciation. A sacred trust rests upon the present generation to hold and transmit the inheritance of the pioneer fathers, their broad and productive acres, the institutions of education, morality and religion, which they established and so faithfully maintained, and their personal character, moral worth and religious hopes, so that unborn generations will arise and call them blessed.

BIBLIOGRAPHY

Pictorial Cincinnati, by Daniel Drake. 1815.

Report of the Commissioner of Common Schools for the year 1854, by H. H. Barney, commissioner; Page 21, one paragraph on the first library of Paddy's Run.

Report of the Commissioner of Common Schools for the year 1885; Pages 50-53, by Jacob P. Sharkey, principal, New London Special District.

Ohio Church History Society Papers, Vol. 10, 1899; Pages 80-100. History of Paddy's Run Congregational Church, by C. A. Gleason.

Ohio Journal of Archeological and Historical Publications. Vol. 16. Pages 198-203 on Paddy's Run, by William Harvey Jones.

The Craftsman; Vol. 20, No. 4; Pages 418-420, July, 1911. The Work of an Old-time Craftsman, by S. R. Williams.

Ohio Journal of Archeological and Historical Publications; Vol. 21 (1912), Pages 462-465, Libraries of Paddy's Run, by S. R. Williams.

Punchard's History of Congregationalism, Vol. 5; Pages 177-185.

Ohio State Medical Journal, Vol. 39, No. 11, Pages 1029-1031 for November, 1943. A Localized Outbreak of Asiatic Cholera in 1834, by S. R. Williams.

INDEX

Abbott, Mrs., 56, 59
Aberle, Clarissa Scott, 64
Abraham, John, 80
Adams, Martha Evans, 139
Adams, William, 56
Adams, Mrs. William, 56
Agnew, Brant, 131
Agnew, David, 132
Amiss, J. Milton, 98
Appleton, Abel, 55, 58, 132
Appleton, Abel, Jr., 79
Appleton, Elizabeth, 113
Appleton, James, 95
Appleton, Thomas, 127, 128
Assel, Rev. John, 120
Assel, Rev. Valentine, 120
Atherton, Belinda, 96
Atherton, David, 127
Atherton, Mary, 96
Atherton, Naomi, 96
Atherton, William, 101, 127
Audubon, J. J., 47

Bails, Foster, 55, 58
Baker, George, 119
Baker, Mrs., 59
Barns, Lydia, 56, 59
Barrows, Henry T., 56
Bebb and Graham, 28
Bebb, Edward, 18, 20, 24, 33, 49, 64, 131, 132, 133, 141
Bebb, Evan, 28
Bebb, Evan R., 99, 133
Bebb, James E., 79
Bebb, Margaret, 19, 141
Bebb, Mary, 141
Bebb, Michael Schuck, 27, 28
Bebb, Sarah, 26
Bebb school, 23
Bebb, Thomas, 79

Bebb, Governor William, 20, 21, 22, 25, 33, 54, 77, 91, 96, 127, 131, 146
Bebb, William (Rhiwgriafol), 50
Beecher, Lyman, 75, 108, 109
Bell, David, 58, 59
Bell, Frank W., 96
Bell, James T., 79
Bell, John W., 94
Bell, Mrs. Margaret, 55, 59
Bevin, John, 80
Bevis, Jesse, 75
Bickley, Ben, 92
Bickley, James, 97
Bickley, U. F., 92
Bissiers, Martin, 55, 58
Black, William, 80, 117
Bottenburg, Daniel, 47
Bottenburg, Dr., 54, 58
Boyd, Gaston, 94
Braun, Laurence, 119
Breese, Richard, 80
Breese, William, 79
Brenan, old Mrs., 59
Brightwell, Mrs. Mary, 140
Brooks, Dr. Peter, 79, 150
Brosey, Hattie-Belle, 157
Brown, Joseph, 132
Brown, L. D., 85
Brown, Stanley W., 96
Brown, W. L., 79
Browne, Rev. John W., 125
Buffington, Jeremiah, 132
Butterfield, Amy, 157
Butterfield, Bryan, 157
Butterfield, Elijah, 157
Butterfield, Jeremiah, 72
Butterfield, Supply, 100
Butterworth, Benjamin, 85, 86

Campbell, Charles R., 95
Campbell, James C., 86, 87
Carmack, Ephraim, 55, 132
Carmack, Mrs., 59
Carter, A. W. C., 23
Case, C. C., 117
Clark, Burkert, 95
Clark, David, 98
Clark, Hugh Williams, 101
Clark, James A., 79
Chidlaw, Rev. B. W., 29, 31, 63, 78, 85, 89, 105, 121, 123, 127, 146, 157, 159
Churchill, Mr., 117
Cisle, John, 75
Clawson, Mrs. Leslie M., 159
Clawson, Dorothy, 99
Colborn, Earl F., 102
Colborn, Sarah, 155
Cone, Hugh, 160
Cone, Miss, 59
Conley, Miss, 59
Conley, Samuel, 55, 58
Corwin, Governor Thomas, 27
Corey, Samuel, 56
Crockett, Davy, 110
Crockett, Mrs. Sarah Woodruff, 109
Cruson, Mr., 66

Dantreece, Hartman, 131
Davidson, Mrs., 107
Davies, Ann, 141
Davies, David E., 110
Davies, David W., 80
Davies, Evan, 42, 110
Davies, Morgan, 79
Davies, Owen P., 95
Davies, Thomas, 79
Davis, Abner F., 79
Davis, Evan, 96
Davis, John, 41, 93
Davis, Hampton, 25
Davis, William, 41
Davis, William B., 41, 93
Day, Mr., 50, 59
Dean, Joseph, 108

Dean, Julia, 56
DeArmond, A. W., 79
DeArmond, Clarence, 101
DeArmond, James, 79
DeArmond, J. T., 79
DeArmond, W. Ross, 102
Dennison, Governor William, 24
Dick, Samuel, 72
Doelker, Jacob, 119
Doelker, Killian, 119
Doelker, Samuel F., 98
Douglass, Emma D., 97
Dowd, Mary, 56
Doyle, Mr., 56
Drake, Dr. Daniel, 51, 56, 57
Dusenberry, William A., 79, 80
Duvall, A. W., 93
Duvall, Ella, 98
Duvall, Lawrence B., 98
Duvall, Matthew, 97
Duvall, William R., 98

Ent, Major Charles, 78, 148
Ent, Miss, 55, 59
Ent, Mr., 55
Ephraim Carmack society, 72
Erven, Isaac, 79
Evans, Albert, 94
Evans, Eliza, 110
Evans, Edward N., 92
Evans, Evan, 128
Evans, Harry, 127
Evans, John, 99, 153, 161
Evans, John B., 80
Evans, John D., Jr., 101
Evans, John J., 79
Evans, John L., 83, 84, 88, 100
Evans, John O., 79
Evans, Mabel, 98
Evans, Martha, 99
Evans, Mattie, 97
Evans, Minor, 101
Evans, Rees H., 80, 141
Evans, Robert, 155
Evans, Sarah, 153
Evans, Spencer E., 90, 123
Evans, William C., 80

INDEX

195

Evans, William G., 80
Evans, William V., 101

Fandree, Mrs., 59
Fenton, John, 108
Firestone, Clark B., 146
French, Jeremiah, 55, 59
French, Mr., 55, 59
Francis, Abner, 107, 128, 160
Francis, Captain Abner, 47, 77
Francis, David, 108, 160
Francis, David and Mary, 18
Francis, Edward, 30, 95, 112
Francis, Eliza, 97
Francis, Elizabeth, 160
Francis, Florence, 131
Francis, John, 94
Francis, Mark, 30, 95, 96, 112
Francis, Roland D., 102

Gause, John T., 56
George, J. Frank, 94
Gilber, Colonel A. W., 78
Gilliland, Adam, 64
Gilliland, James, 64
Glancy, Josephine, 148
Gleason, C. A., 121
Goshorn, J. A., 97
Graham, Edward C., 133
Graveyard surnames, 113
Griffith, Daniel, 79
Griffith, David, 66
Griffith, Evan, 80
Griffith, John, 80
Griffith, Richard, 79
Groesbeck, Colonel John, 78
Groesbeck, W. S., 56
Guthrie, Alex, 83
Guthrie, John, 100
Gwilym, Morgan, 41, 71, 110, 113

Halderman, Mr., 66
Hall, Henry, 79
Halstead, Benton, 92, 109
Halstead, Colonel Griffin, 77, 84, 109, 145, 146
Halstead, John, 64, 131, 144, 145, 146

Halstead, John, Jr., 93
Halstead, Murat, 17, 29, 87, 102, 109, 121, 145, 146
Halstead, Sarah, 145
Harding, Emily W., 91
Harvey, Asa, 72
Hawk, Mr., 122
Hawk, Rev. Jacob, 122
Hayden, Stephen, 63
Hemingway, Mary W., 91
Hepburn, President A. D., 106
Hickory chapel of Rees Lloyd, 74, 75
Hidlay, old Mr., 55, 58
Hidlay, old Mrs., 55, 59
Hidlay, young Mrs., 55, 59
Hieatt, Carrie, 86
Hindman, Miss, 56, 59
Hindman, Mrs., 56, 59
Hoadly, George, 85, 86
Hornick, David, 131
Howell, Evan, 79
Howell, Sam, 80
Hughes, Ezekiel, 18, 19, 159
Hughes, Richard L., 80
Humes, Clarence M., 92
Hyde, Mr., 72

Iseminger, George, 71
Iseminger, John, 71
Irwin, Clara W., 99, 154
Irwin, Raymond, 157

James, Henry, 102
Jarvis, Richard, 50
Johnston, Judge W. T., 27
Jones, Abner F., 84, 89
Jones, Andrew J., 79
Jones, Ann, 157
Jones, Anna B., 91, 145
Jones, Bachgen, 81
Jones, Betsy, 160
Jones, Edward H., 92
Jones, Edward T., 79
Jones, Etta, 144
Jones, Griffith M., 66
Jones, James W., 80

Jones, Israel, 80
Jones, Squire John C., 141, 160
Jones, John H., 80
Jones, John J., 80
Jones, John L., 79
Jones, John W., 80
Jones, Mary, 157
Jones, Mary C., 160
Jones, Mattie D., 97
Jones, Maurice, 55, 58, 79
Jones, Mrs. Maurice, 55, 59
Jones, Michael, 79, 96, 156
Jones, Morris S., 80
Jones, Oliver, 97
Jones, Mrs. Parthena W., 142
Jones, William D., 132
Jones, William F., 94, 95

Kelshymer, Francis, 66
Kilburn, Mr., 135
Kingsley, Dr., 55
Kinney, Tom, 119
Knauss, Peter, Sr., 119
Koger, J. Kenneth, 99

Langridge, Clarinda W., 90
Langridge, John, 156
Larrabee, Charles, 24
Lewis, Andrew, 31
Lewis, Bill, 111
Lewis, Dave, 111
Lewis, William, 79
Lewis, William T., 79, 80, 89, 107, 108
Little, John, 120
Lloyd, Benjamin, 72, 124
Lloyd, David, 21
Lloyd, Rees, 18, 124
Longworth, Nicholas, 41
Lyle, Squire Benny, 117

Manuel, John S., 100
Manuel, Richard, 80, 81
Manuel, William, 80
Manuel, William S., 100
Marsh, Moses, 112
Martin, A. W., 123

Martindal, A., 108
Matson, John, 160
Mauer, Robert S., 102
Melindy, Peter, 25
Mercer, Wilson, 108
Mering, David, 79
Mering, George, 113
Mering, John, 47
Milholland, David, 94
Milholland, George, 113
Milholland, John, 80, 93
Milholland, William, 93, 94
Milholland, W. L., 79
Miller, Emeline, 156
Miller, Laurence, 119
Millikin, Brigadier General R. B., 79
Monfort, J. G., 56
Moore, E., 56
Morgan, Ann, 110
Morgan, John O., 80
Morris, A. Gilson, 79
Morris, Mrs. Anna Chidlaw, 108, 159, 160
Morris, Benjamin Chidlaw, 102, 106
Morris, Crawford Minter, 160
Morris, Edith, 98, 159
Morris, Griffith, 128, 146, 159
Morris, Evan, Jr., 100, 159
Morris, Evan, Sr., 159
Morris, Homer, 92, 159
Morris, Jane, 159
Morris, John, 159
Morris, John H., 80, 108
Morris, Mary Jane Wasson, 159
Morris, Minor, 94, 159
Morris, Minter Crawford, 108, 122, 159
Morris, Thomas, 50
Morris, Thomas M., 80
Morris, Walter, 159
Murray, Captain, 79

McBride, Francis, 80
McBride, James, 73
McClelland, Isaac, 64, 143, 154
McClelland, Thomas, 90

INDEX

McClelland, Samuel, 96
McClung, D. W., 85
McCune, James, 131
McCune, William, 131
McHenry, O. P., 94
McKasson, Fred D., 78
McKasson, Martin, 79

Nicholas, David, 50, 106
Nicholas, James, 105, 106, 127
Nicholas, James, Jr., 47, 49, 92, 106
Nicholas, Martha, 105
Nicholas, Mary Morris, 105, 106
Nicholas, Mary Jones, 50
Nicholas, Richard J., 79

Oldfather, Jeremiah, 117
Owens, David, 131, 153
Owens, Margaret Roberts, 20
Owens, Rev. Mr., 19, 20
Owens, Thomas, 78

Parkinson, Mr., 106
Pastors of Congregational church, 125, 126
Patton, George, 75
Patton, James T., 78, 79, 110
Peabody, Helen, 83
Peate, Anne, 97
Pfeffer, Benedict, 119
Pfotzer, John, 120
Poe, Adam, 34
Postmasters, 88
Pottenger, Joseph L., 95
Pryse, Rev. Mr., 84
Pulse, Peter, 132

Quinlan, Mary I., 99

Ray, James Brown, 29
Rees, William, 79
Reese, Alice Cary, 102
Reese, Betsy, 141
Reese, John, 80
Reese, Robert, 141
Richards, Giles, 148
Rittenhouse, Alex, 131
Roberts, David, 49

Roberts, George, 18, 20
Roberts, John T., 79
Roberts, Dr. Joseph, 145, 146
Roberts, Margaret, 19
Roberts, Maurice, 79
Roberts, Thomas S., 93
Robinson, Alice Scott, 145, 146
Robinson, C. Kirby, 101
Robinson, Erastus, 94
Robinson, Henry, Sr., 145, 149
Robinson, Henry Halstead, 146
Robinson, Henry Hidlay, 148
Robinson, Mrs. H. H., 128
Robinson, Mary M., 97
Robinson, Paul, 102
Robinson, Samuel, 148
Robinson, Virginia, 146
Robeson, Mrs., 55, 59
Ross, Carmen, 59
Ross, David, 108
Rothermel, Jessie, 157
Rowland, Richard, 80
Rowland, Stanley, 97, 98
Rude, Reuben, 59
Rust, Mr., 58

Sater, Clinton H., 96
Sater, John Elbert, 92
Sater, Lowry F., 92, 112
Schaefer, Michael, 119
Scheel, Jacob, 119, 128
Scheel, Charles, 101
Scheel, Orsini, 94, 108
Scheel, Thomas J. J., 100
Scheering, John, 119
Scheering, Mathias, 119
Schradin, Leslie J., 95
Schradin, Stanley, 102
Schradin, William, 93
Schultz, Mrs. Elizabeth Thomas Owens, 136
Scott, Benton Halstead, 94
Scott, E. Walter, 90
Scott, Hally Mering, 102
Scott, Harry T., 108
Scott, Helen Halstead, 145
Scott, Rev. Hugh, 108

Scott, James, 101
Scott, James, 79
Scott, Deacon J. C., 56, 59
Scott, John M., 145
Scott, John Marshall, 95
Scott, Rebecca, 56
Scott, Warner B., 96
Scott, W. Ernest, 101
Sefton, Henry, 55, 59
Sharkey, J. P., 133
Shaw, Albert, 29, 102, 106, 112, 121, 135, 153
Shaw, Albin, 79
Shaw, Daniel, 25
Shaw, Esquire, 72
Shaw, Griffin M., 25, 84, 93
Shaw, Dr. Griffin McKendree, 153
Shaw, G. M., Jr., 153
Shaw, Hezekiah, 112
Shaw, John Fletcher, 93
Shaw, Lucy, 153
Shaw, Mary, 153
Shaw, Knowles, 72
Shaw, Roger, 112
Shields, David, 145
Shields, James, 20, 127, 132, 141
Shields, Jane, 143
Shields, Matthew R., 100
Shields, Thomas J., 47
Sizelove, Mr., 58
Sizelove, Mrs., 59
Sizelove, Wilford, 98
Slingsby, Keiday, 55, 58
Smith, Hugh, 77, 132
Sonnentag, Thaddeus, 119
Squirrel hunt prize donors, 46
Starlin, Charles E., 101
Starr, Clayton H., 99
Starr, Gordon G., 98
Stevenson, Adlai, 87

Talmage, Rev. L. C., 123
Taylor, W. H. H., 79
Teachers, academy, 128
Teachers, grade school, 128, 129
Teetor, Carl, 93
Teetor, Paul, 102

Thomas, Alfred, 92
Thomas, Evan B., 80
Thomas, Rev. Thomas, 21, 22, 108, 124, 125, 147
Thomas, Mrs. Thomas, 147
Thomas, Thomas A., 79
Thomas, Thomas E., 29, 56, 89
Thomas, Dr. William, No. 1, 147
Thomas, Dr. William, No. 2, 147, 148
Thompson, President W. O., 30, 121, 123
Tomkins, Rev. Seely K., 122
Tudor, William W., 80
Tweedy, Elizabeth W., 90
Tweedy, James, 156

Van Vickle, Ephraim, 55, 58
Vaughan, John, 105, 113, 132, 140
Vaughan, John Green, 141
Vaughan, Martha, 140
Vaughan, Martha Ann, 141
Vaughan, Mrs. Mary Bebb, 51, 141, 146
Vaughan, William, 83, 140, 141
Vaughan, William Crosby, 14, 79
Venable, Ann, 55, 59
Venable, Mr., 58
Volweiler, Albert, 98

Waer, James S., 131
Walther, Fred, 119
Walther, John, 119, 120
Watkins, Evan R., 80
Watkins, Thomas, 49
Welwood, Rev. S. D., 122
Wilds, Edward, 102
Wiley, Miss Polly, 127
Wilkins, Daniel, 144
Wilkins, John, 90, 157
Willey, Noah, 72
Williams, Hugh, 112, 127, 149, 153
Williams, Mark, 29, 83, 89, 134
Williams, Roger, 83, 106, 107, 112
Wilson, Rev. David, 125
Wilson, Rev. Samuel T., 96
Woodruff, Daniel, 109

Woodruff, John, 54, 58, 109
Woodruff, Lillian, 101
Woodruff, Reuben, 54, 109
Woodruff, Samuel W., 79
Wooley, Job, 110

Yaeger, George, 131
Yaeger, Joseph, 131
Youmans, Andrew, Jr., 79

www.ingramcontent.com/pod-product-compliance
Lightning Source LLC
Chambersburg PA
CBHW030326100526
44592CB00010B/587